FOR ORGANS, PIANOS & ELECTRONIC KEYBOARDS

E-Z PLAY® TODAY 163

R&B BALLADS

CONTENTS

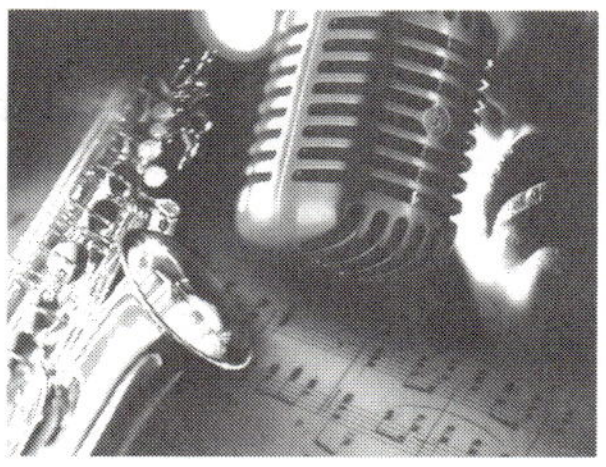

ISBN 0-7935-8232-6

HAL•LEONARD® CORPORATION
7777 W. BLUEMOUND RD. P.O. BOX 13819 MILWAUKEE, WI 53213

Visit Hal Leonard Online at
www.halleonard.com

Ain't No Mountain High Enough

Registration 4
Rhythm: Rock or 8-Beat

Words and Music by Nickolas Ashford
and Valerie Simpson

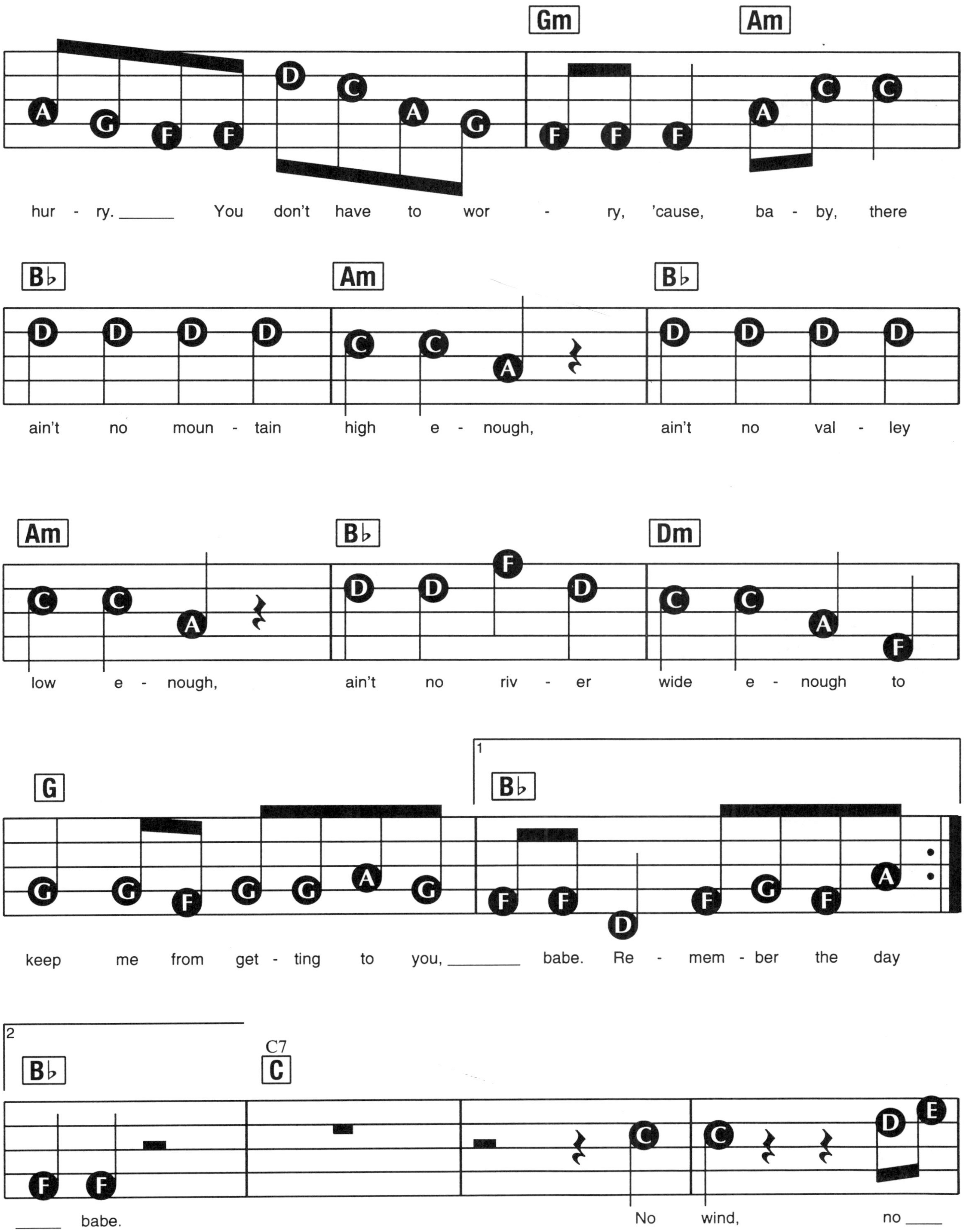
Gm Am
hur - ry. You don't have to wor - ry, 'cause, ba - by, there
B♭ Am B♭
ain't no moun - tain high e - nough, ain't no val - ley
Am B♭ Dm
low e - nough, ain't no riv - er wide e - nough to
G 1 B♭
keep me from get - ting to you, babe. Re - mem - ber the day
2 B♭ C7 C
babe. No wind, no

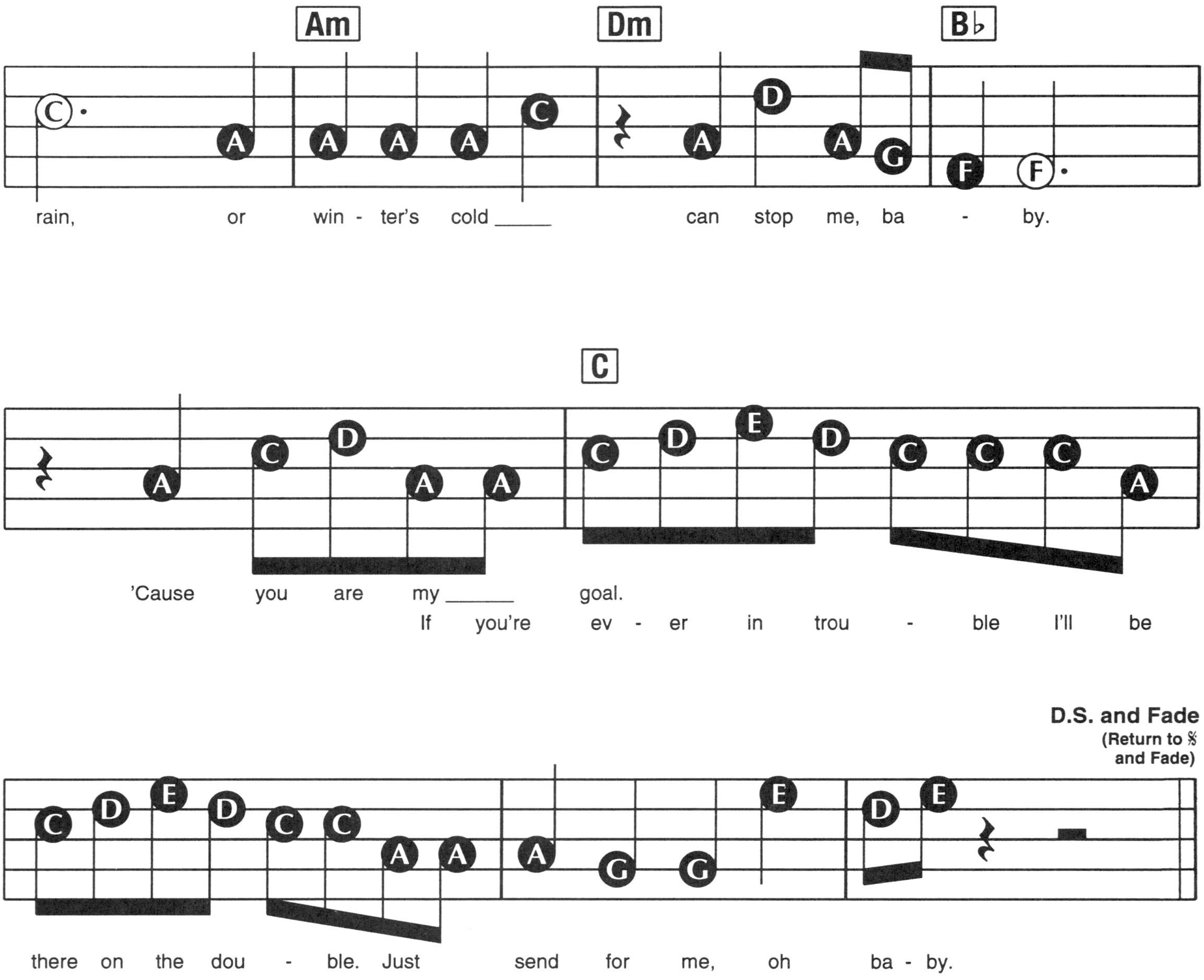

Additional Lyrics

2. I set you free.
   I told you you could always count on me.
   From that day on, I made a vow,
   I'll be there when you want me,
   Some way, somehow.
   'Cause baby there *(Chorus)*

3. My love is alive
   Way down in my heart,
   Although we are miles apart.
   If you ever need a helping hand,
   I'll be there on the double
   As fast as I can.
   Don't you know that there *(Chorus)*

Ain't Nothing Like the Real Thing

Registration 4
Rhythm: Rock or 16-Beat

Words and Music by Nickolas Ashford
and Valerie Simpson

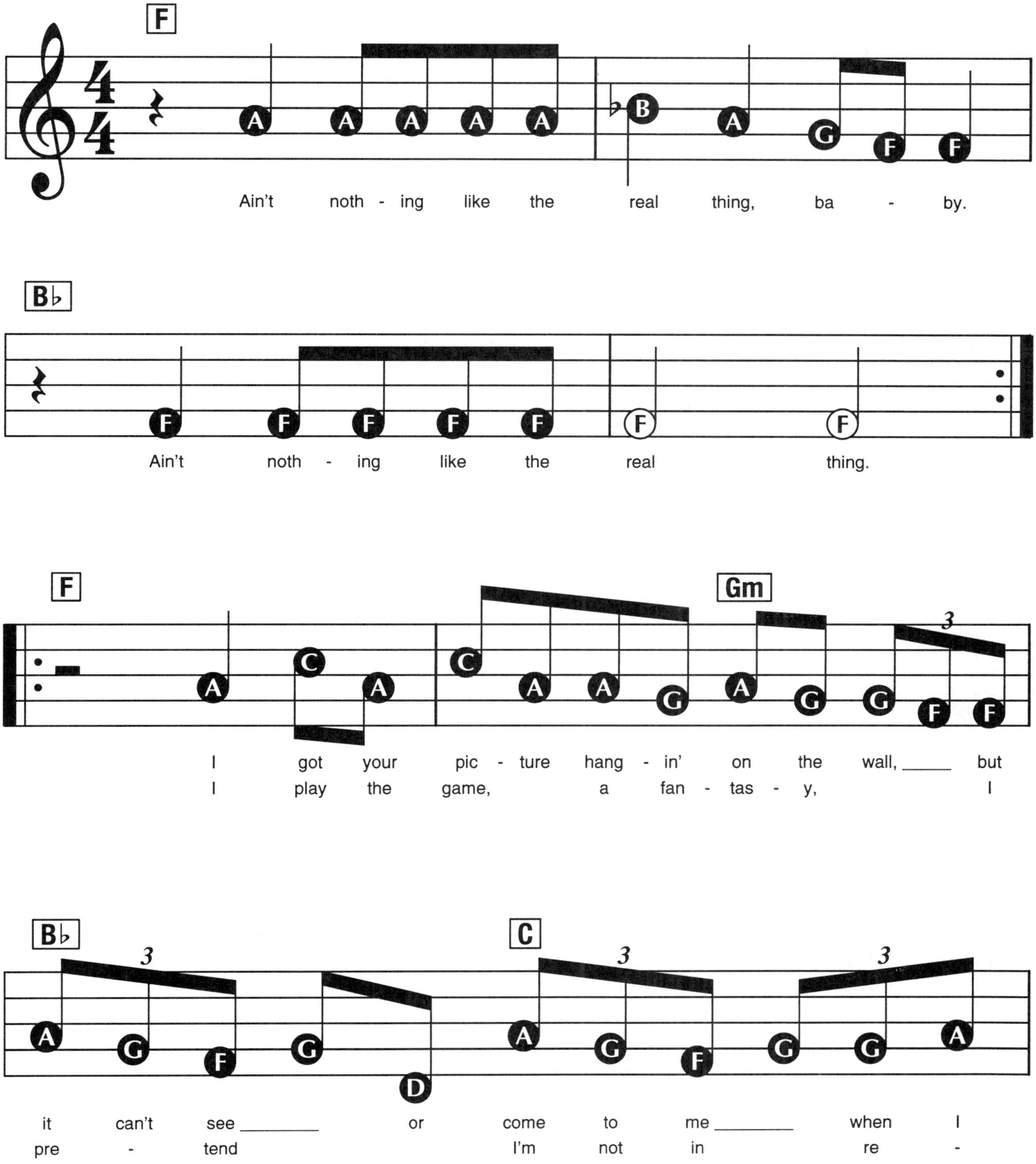

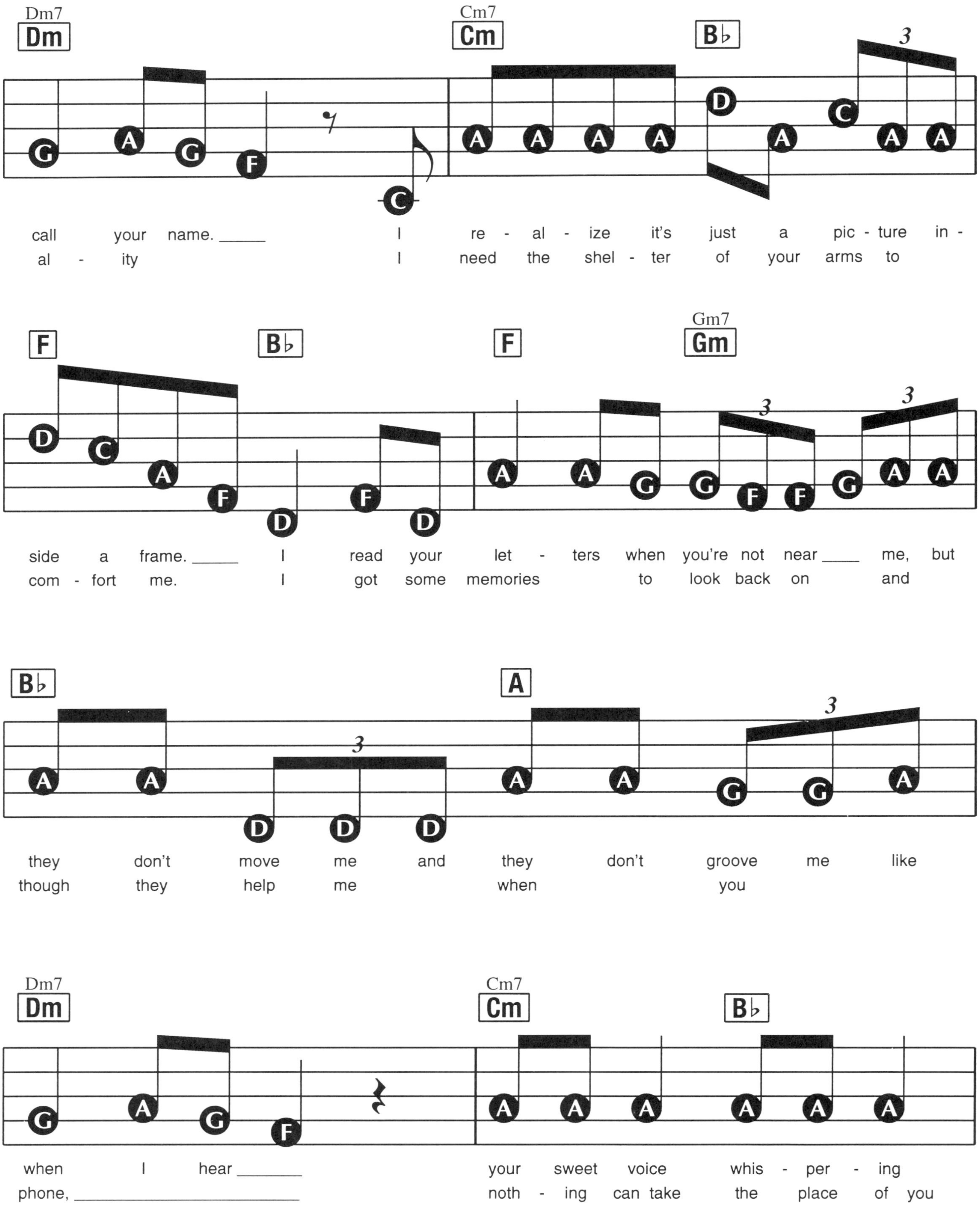
Dm7 Dm
Cm7 Cm
B♭
call your name. _____ I re - al - ize it's just a pic - ture in -
al - ity I need the shel - ter of your arms to
F
B♭
F
Gm7 Gm
side a frame. _____ I read your let - ters when you're not near ____ me, but
com - fort me. I got some memories to look back on and
B♭
A
they don't move me and they don't groove me like
though they help me when you
Dm7 Dm
Cm7 Cm
B♭
when I hear _______ your sweet voice whis - per - ing
phone, _______________________ noth - ing can take the place of you

1
F
B♭
in my ear.
2
F
be - ing there. No oth - er
Am
A
sound is quite the same as your name.
Dm
Cm7
Cm
B♭
No touch can do half as much to
D7
D
Gm7
Gm
C
make me feel bet - ter, so let's get to - geth - er.
D.C. and Fade
(Return to beginning and Fade)

Ben

Registration 1
Rhythm: Pops or 8 Beat

Lyrics by Don Black
Music by Walter Scharf

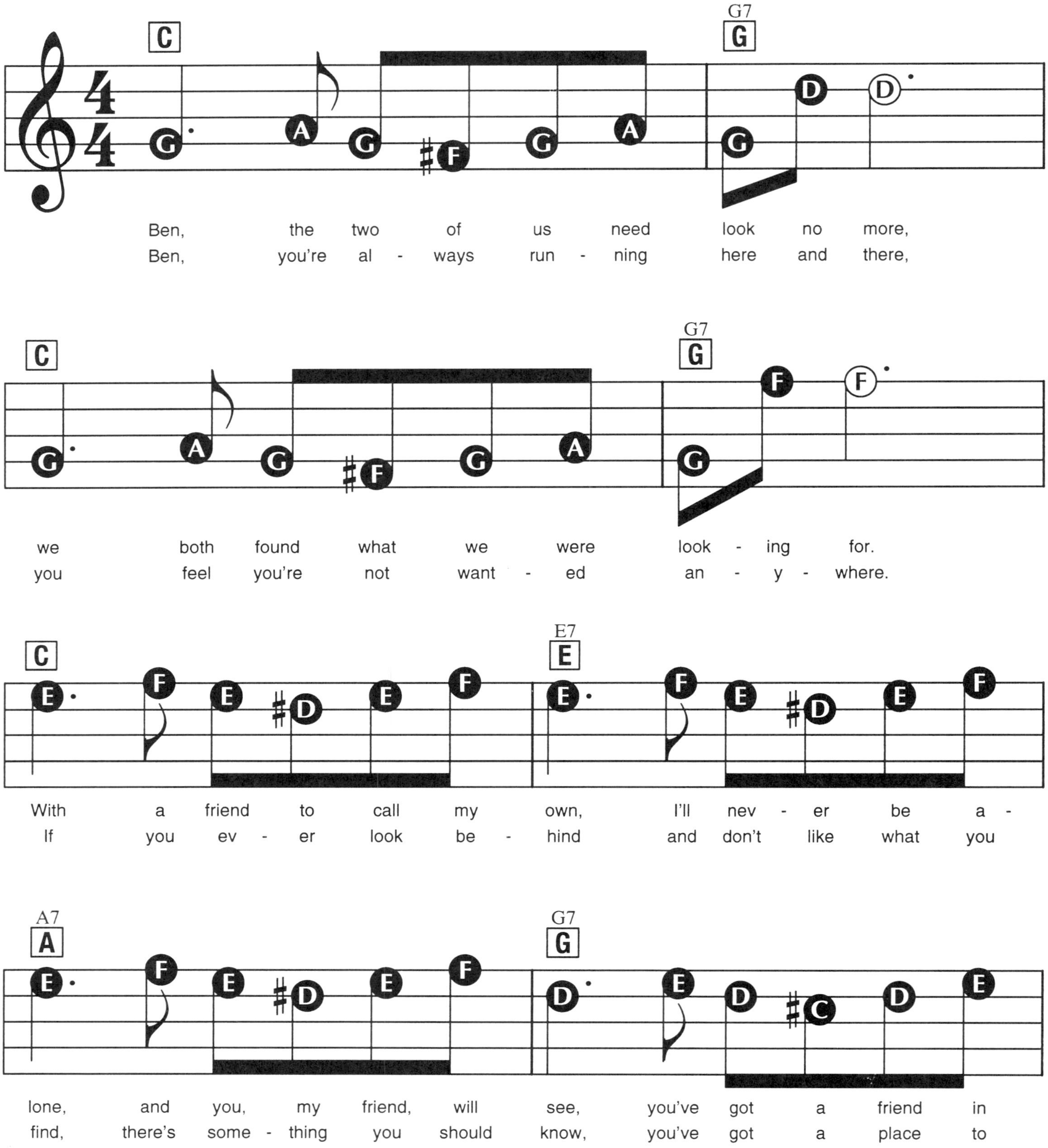

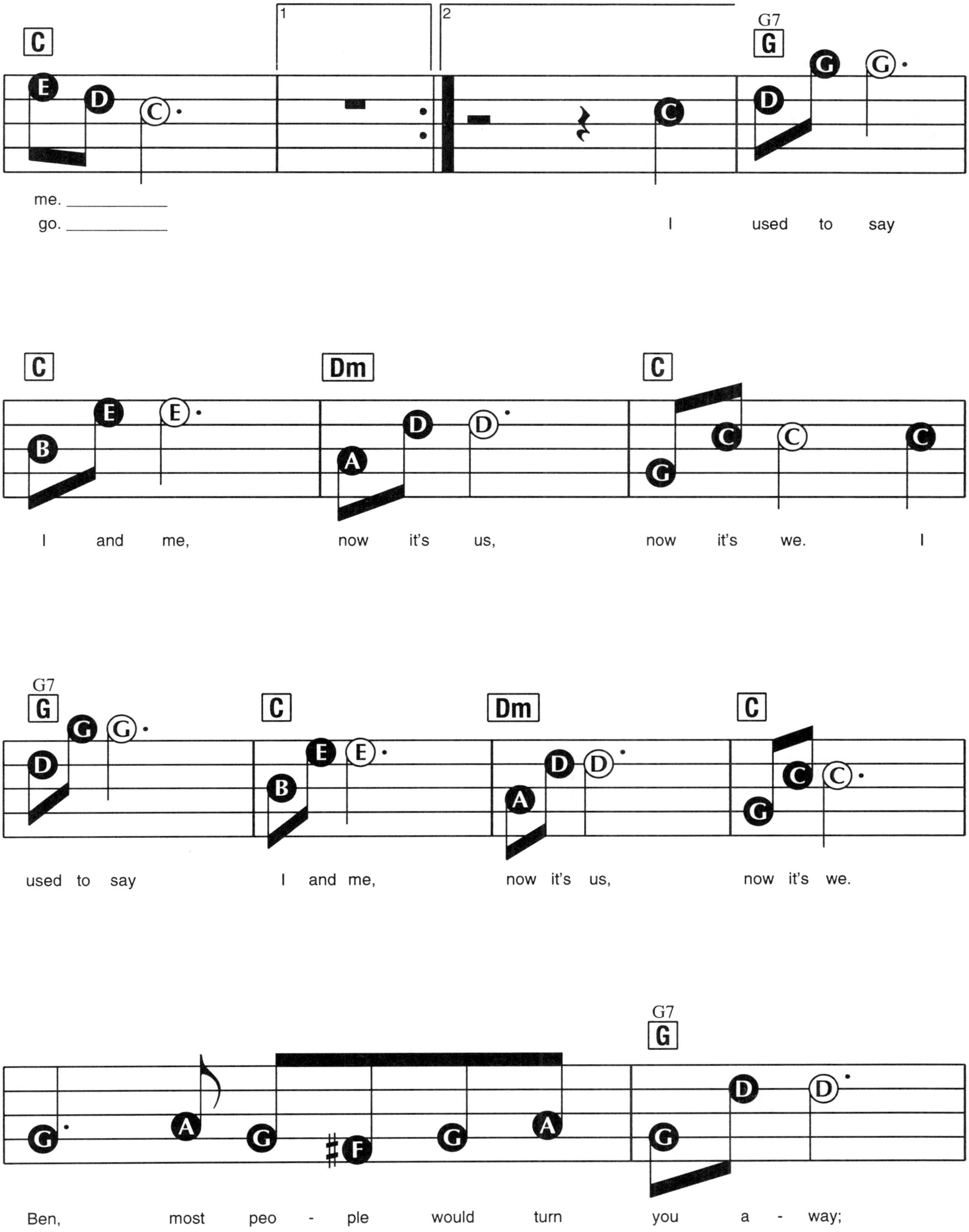
me.
go.
I used to say
I and me, now it's us, now it's we. I
used to say I and me, now it's us, now it's we.
Ben, most peo - ple would turn you a - way;

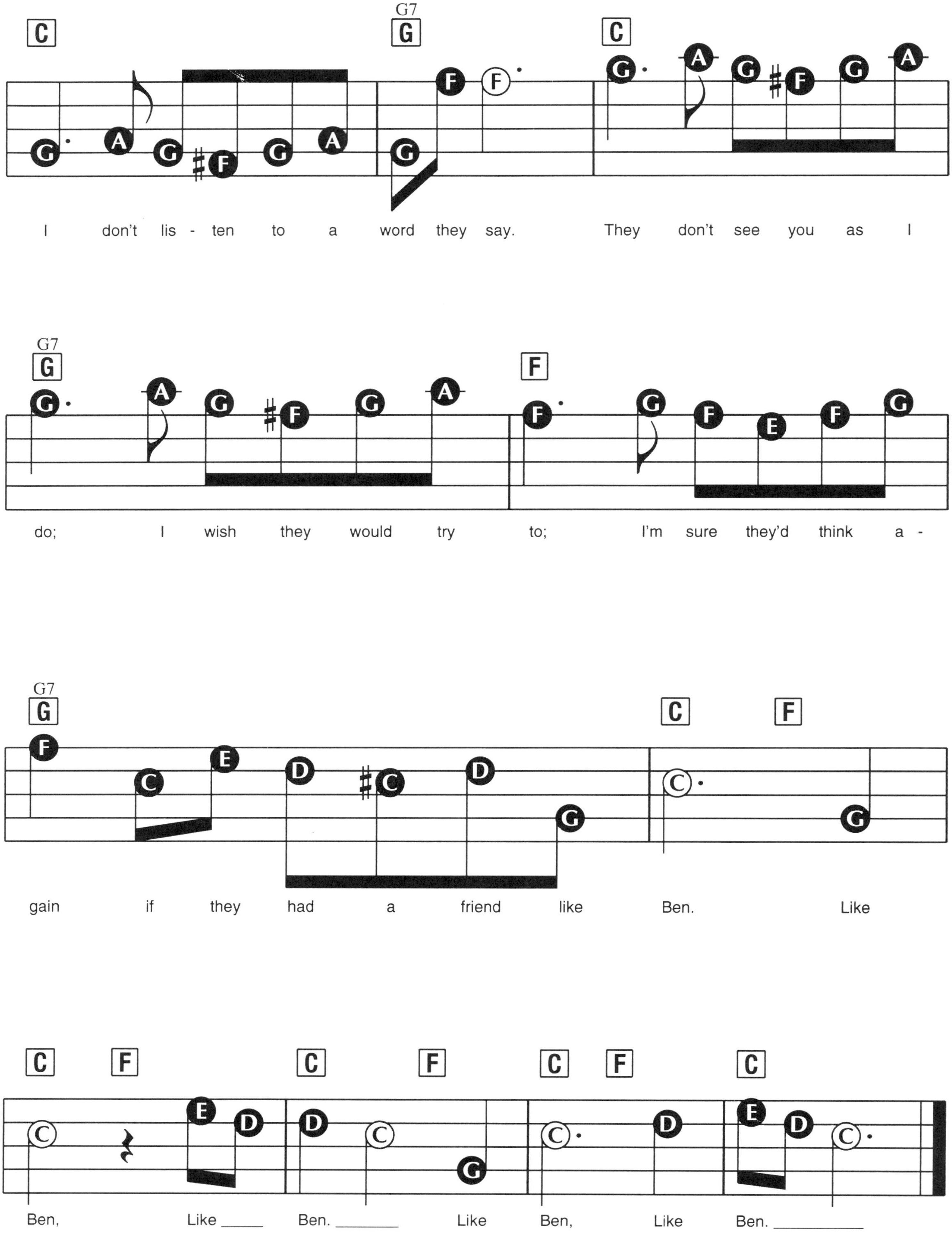
C G7 G C
I don't lis - ten to a word they say. They don't see you as I
G7 G F
do; I wish they would try to; I'm sure they'd think a -
G7 G C F
gain if they had a friend like Ben. Like
C F C F C F C
Ben, Like _____ Ben. ________ Like Ben, Like Ben. ___________

Do You Know Where You're Going To?

Theme from MAHOGANY

Words by Gerry Goffin
Music by Mike Masser

Registration 5
Rhythm: Slow Rock or Ballad

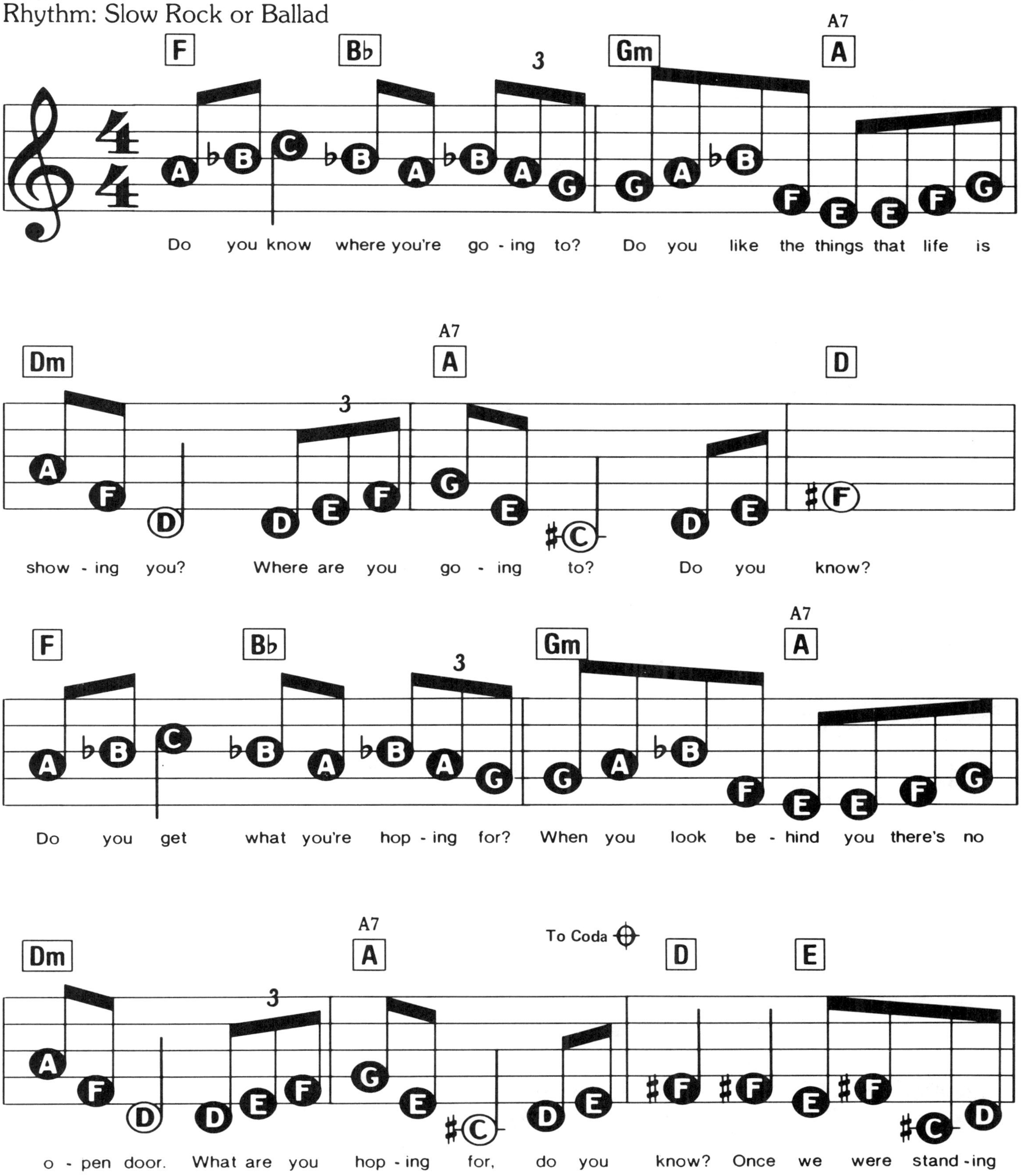

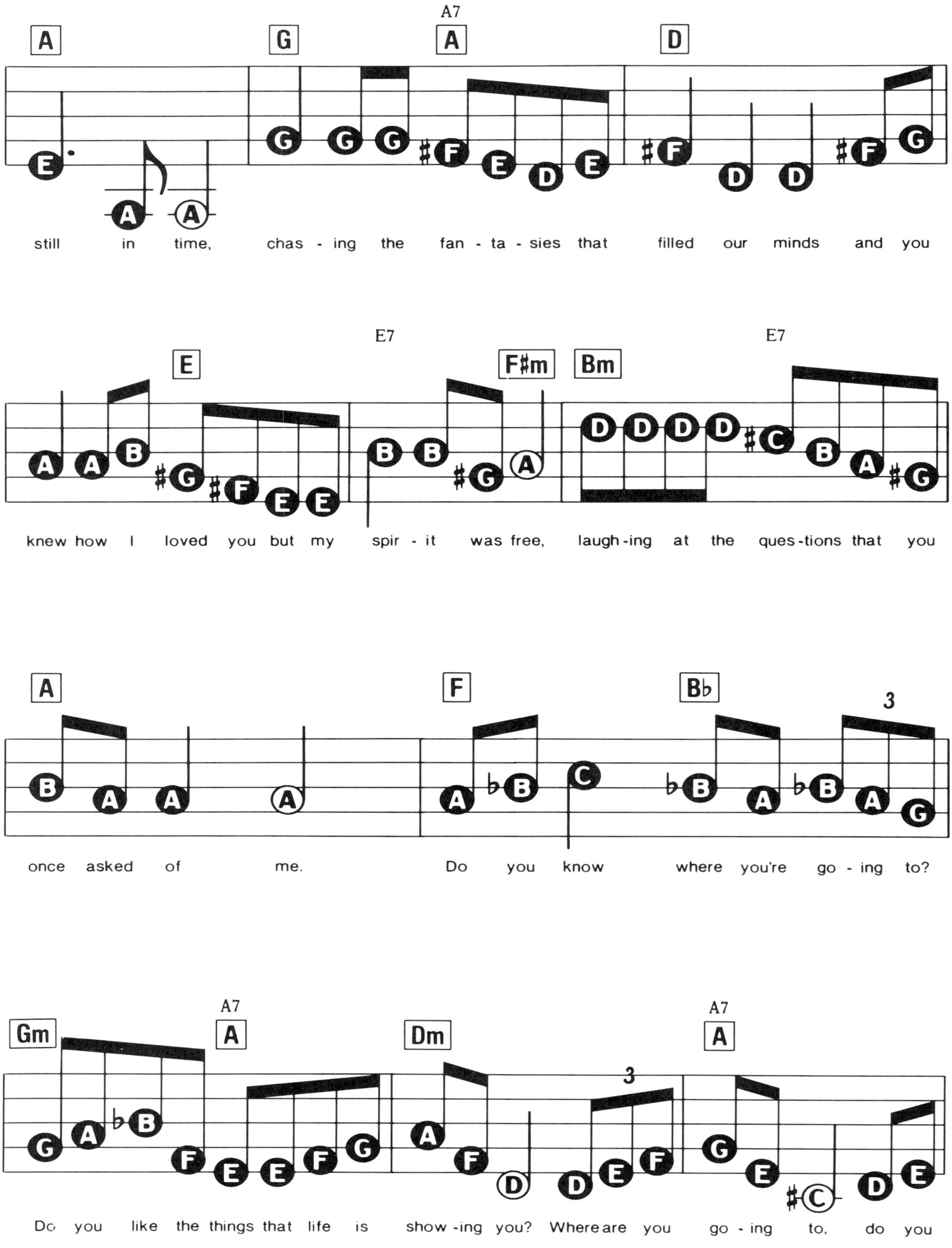
A G A7 A D
still in time, chas - ing the fan - ta - sies that filled our minds and you
E E7 F♯m Bm E7
knew how I loved you but my spir - it was free, laugh - ing at the ques - tions that you
A F B♭ 3
once asked of me. Do you know where you're go - ing to?
Gm A7 A Dm 3 A7 A
Do you like the things that life is show - ing you? Where are you go - ing to, do you

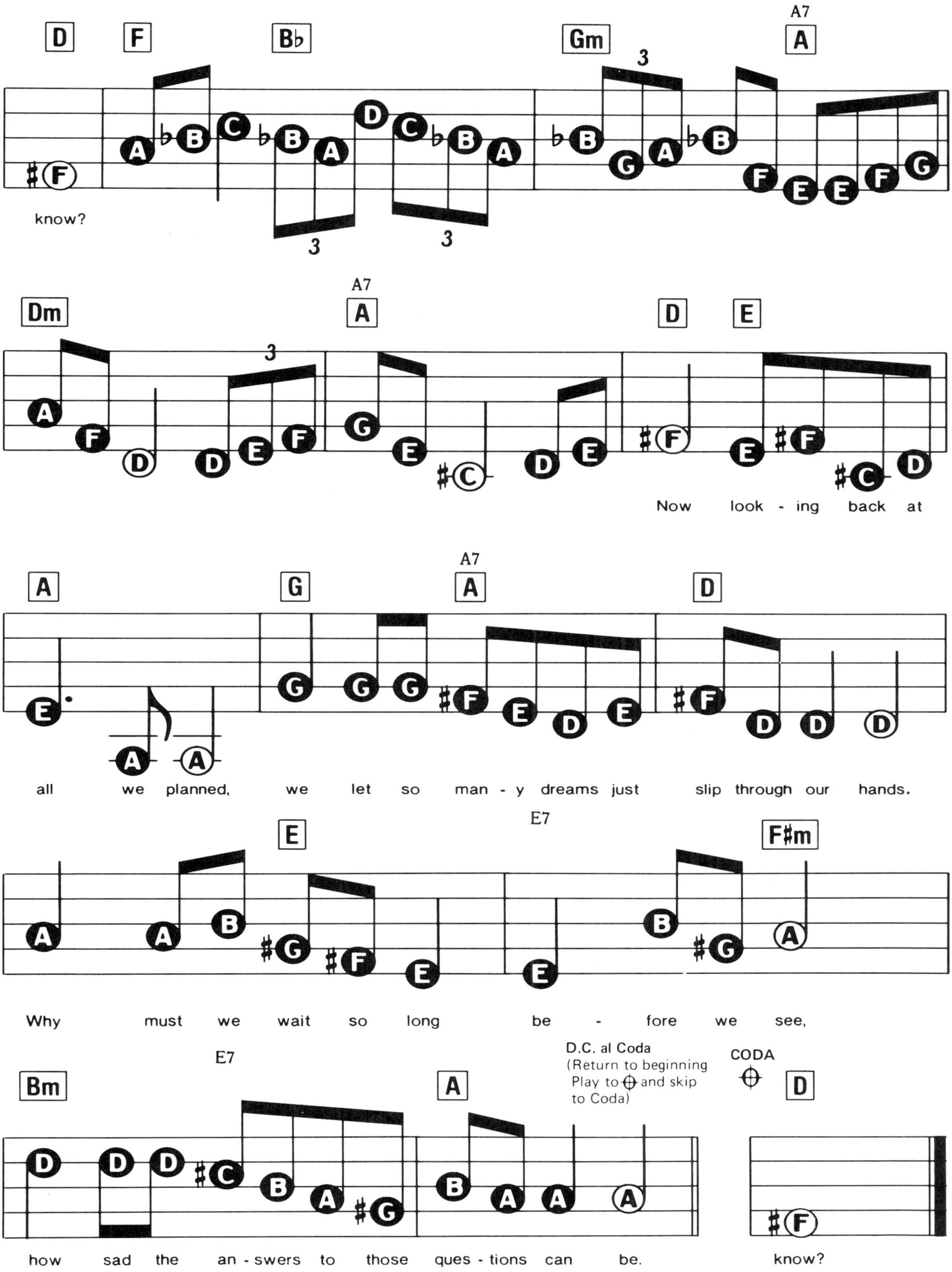
D F B♭ Gm A7 A
know?
Dm A7 A D E
Now look - ing back at
A G A7 A D
all we planned, we let so man - y dreams just slip through our hands.
E E7 F♯m
Why must we wait so long be - fore we see,
Bm E7 A
how sad the an - swers to those ques - tions can be.
D.C. al Coda
(Return to beginning
Play to ⊕ and skip
to Coda)
CODA
D
know?

Easy

Registration 3
Rhythm: Pops or 8 Beat

Words and Music by
Lionel Richie

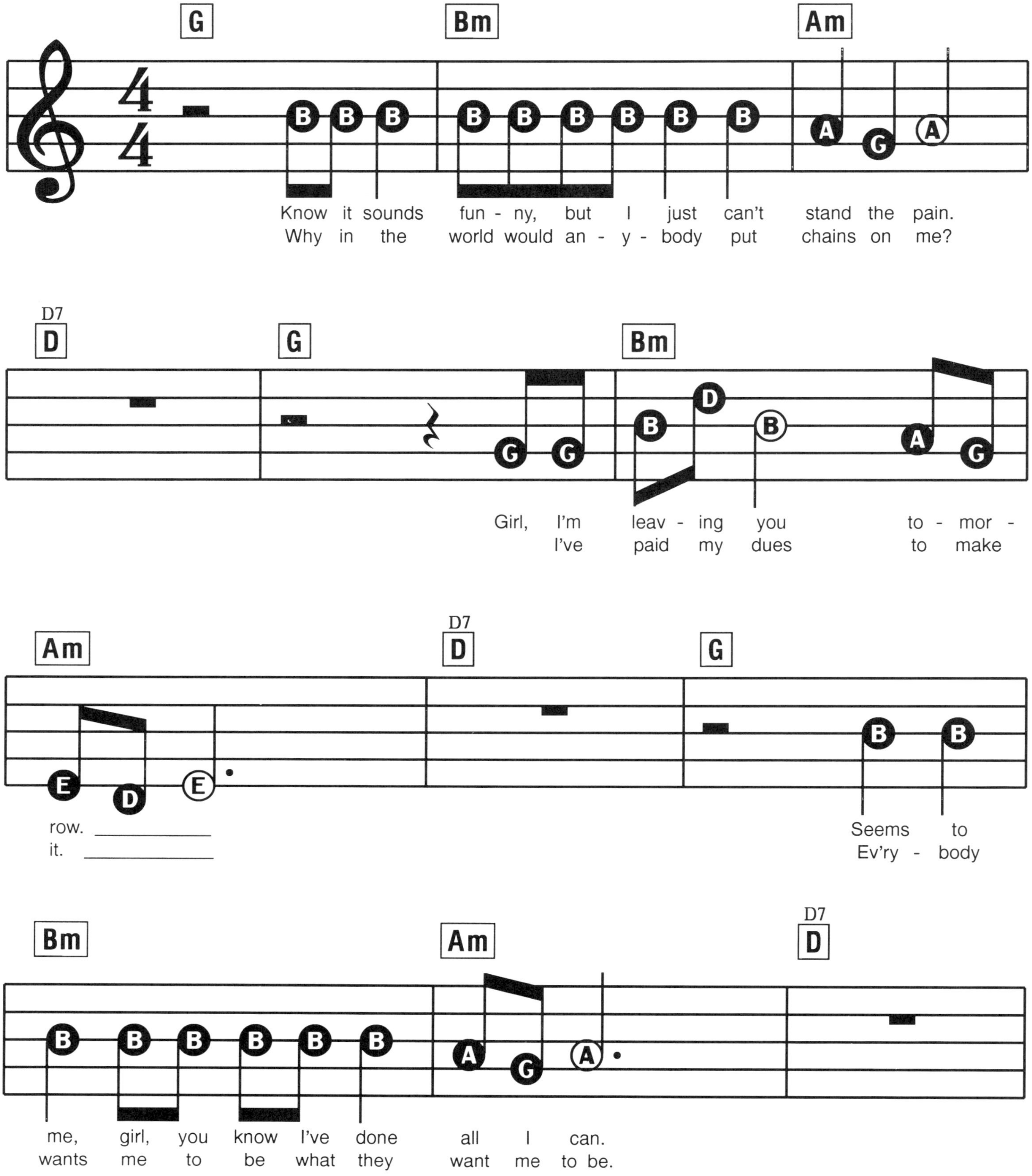

G Bm Am
You see, I begged, stole and I bor - rowed.
I'm not happy when I try to fake it,
D7 D
Yeah, ___ ooh.
no. ___ Ooh.
That's why I'm eas -
G Bm Am
- y, (Ah) ___ I'm
D7 D G Bm
eas - y like Sun - day morn - ing. (Ah) ___
Am D7 D G
___ That's why I'm eas - y, ___

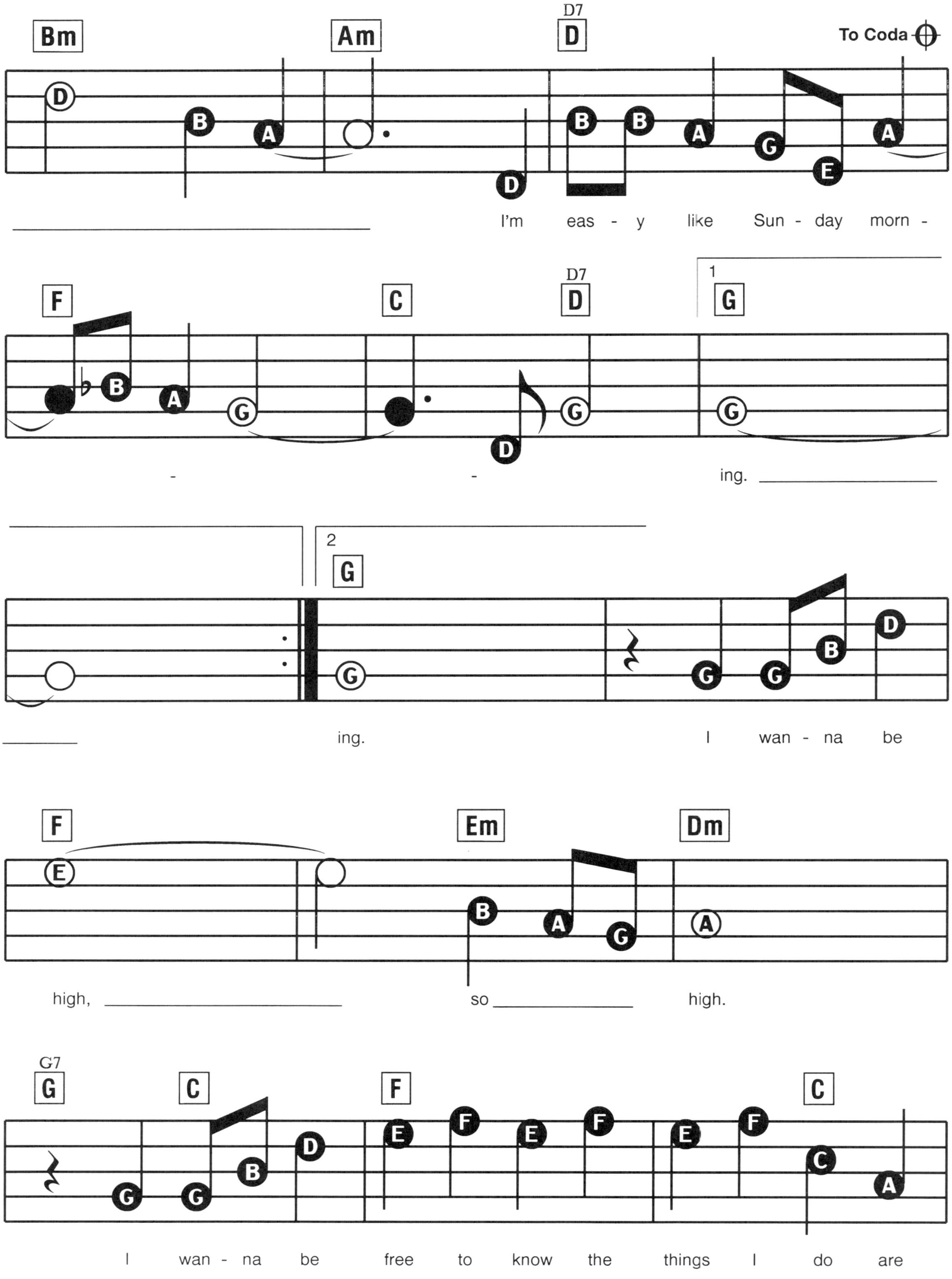
Bm
Am
D7
D
To Coda
I'm eas - y like Sun - day morn -
F
C
D7
D
1
G
- - ing.
2
G
ing.
I wan - na be
F
Em
Dm
high, so high.
G7
G
C
F
C
I wan - na be free to know the things I do are

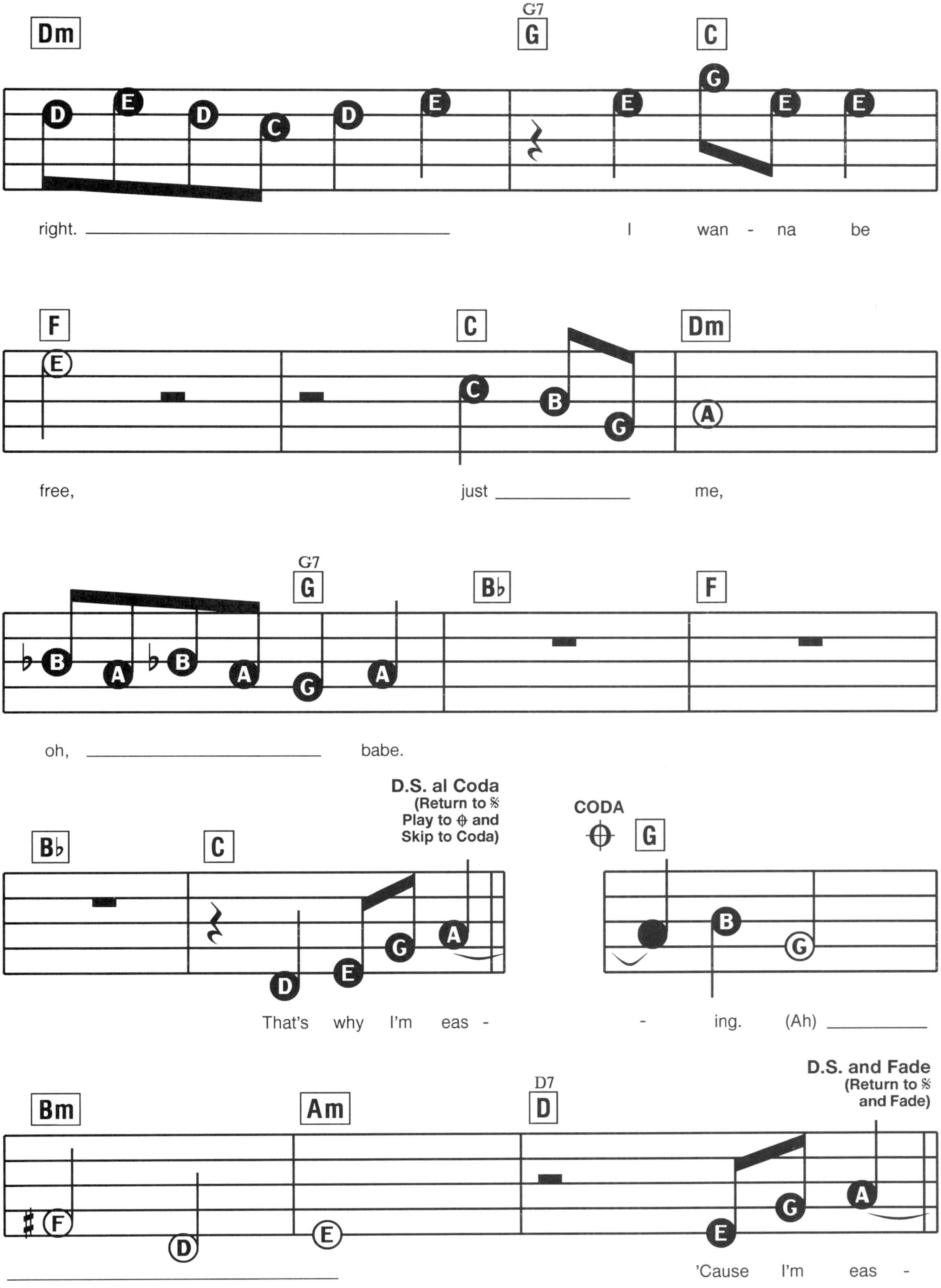
Dm
G7
G
C
D E D C D E E G E E
right. I wan - na be
F
C
Dm
E C B G A
free, just me,
G7
G
B♭
F
B A B A G A
oh, babe.
D.S. al Coda
(Return to 𝄋
Play to ⊕ and
Skip to Coda)
CODA
B♭
C
G
D E G A B G
That's why I'm eas - - ing. (Ah)
D.S. and Fade
(Return to 𝄋
and Fade)
Bm
Am
D7
D
F D E E G A
'Cause I'm eas -

Got to Be There

Registration 1
Rhythm: Rock or 8-Beat

Words and Music by
Elliot Willensky

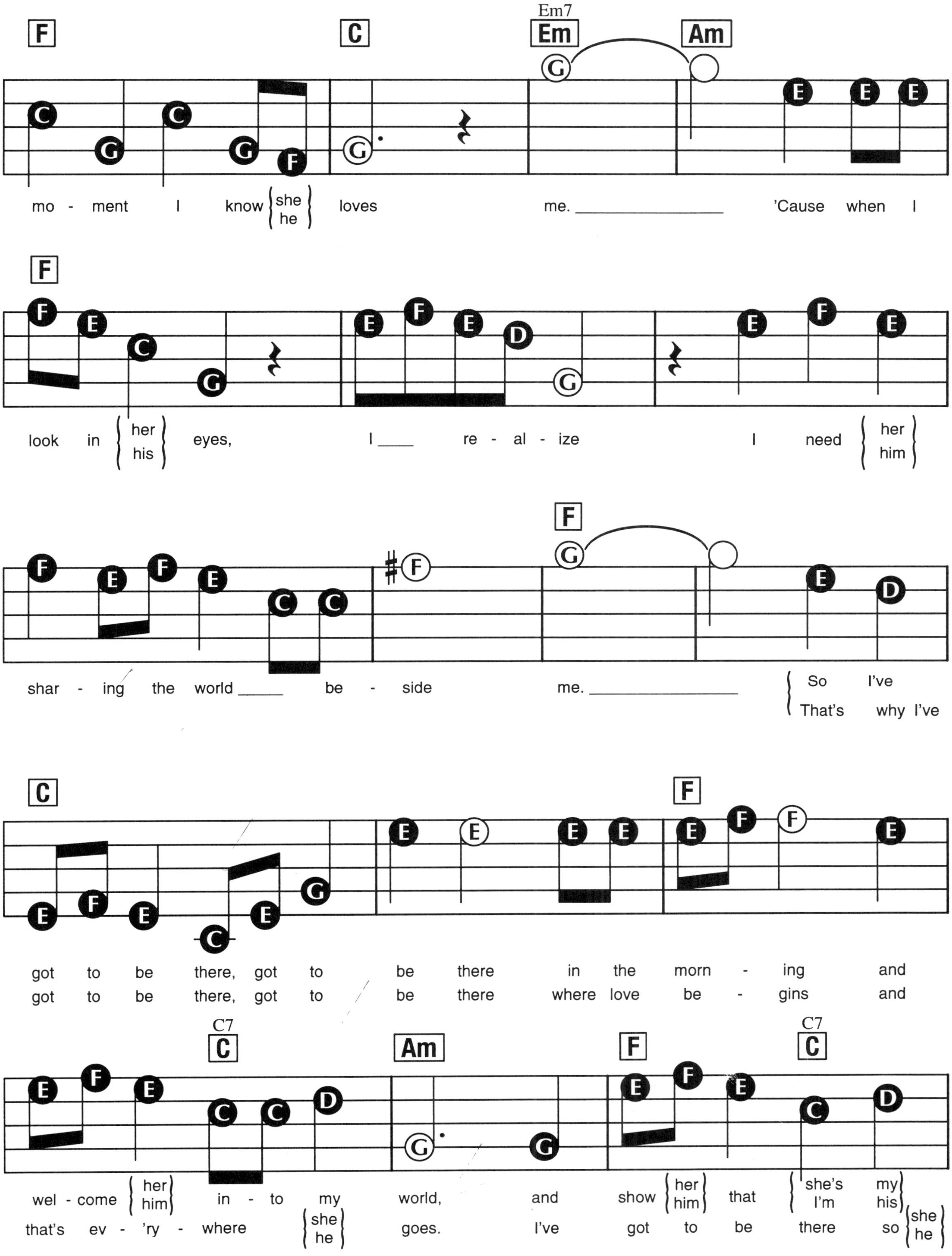
F
C
Em7
Em
Am
C G C G F G G E E E
mo - ment I know {she he} loves me. 'Cause when I
F
F E C G E F E D G E F E
look in {her his} eyes, I re - al - ize I need {her him}
F
F E F E C C F G E D
shar - ing the world be - side me. {So I've / That's why I've}
C
F
E F E C E G E E E E E F F E
got to be there, got to be there in the morn - ing and
got to be there, got to be there where love be - gins and
C7
C
Am
F
C7
C
E F E C C D G G E F E C D
wel - come {her him} in - to my world, and show {her him} that {she's I'm} my{his}
that's ev - 'ry - where {she he} goes. I've got to be there so {she he}

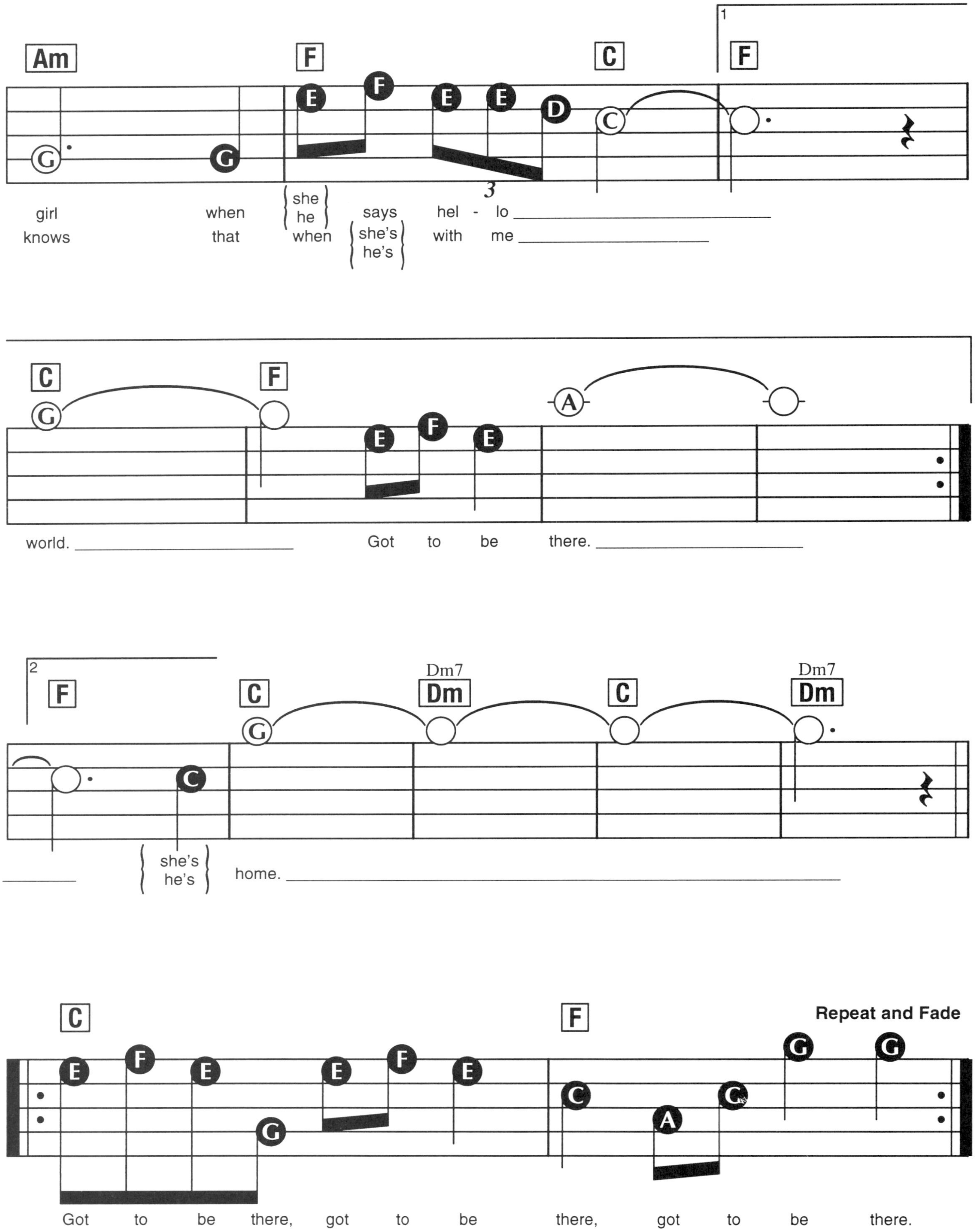
Am
F
C
1
F
girl when she he says hel - lo
knows that when she's he's with me
C
F
world. Got to be there.
2
F
C
Dm7
Dm
C
Dm7
Dm
she's he's home.
C
F
Repeat and Fade
Got to be there, got to be there, got to be there.

I Hear a Symphony

Registration 4
Rhythm: Swing or Shuffle

Words and Music by Edward Holland,
Lamont Dozier and Brian Holland

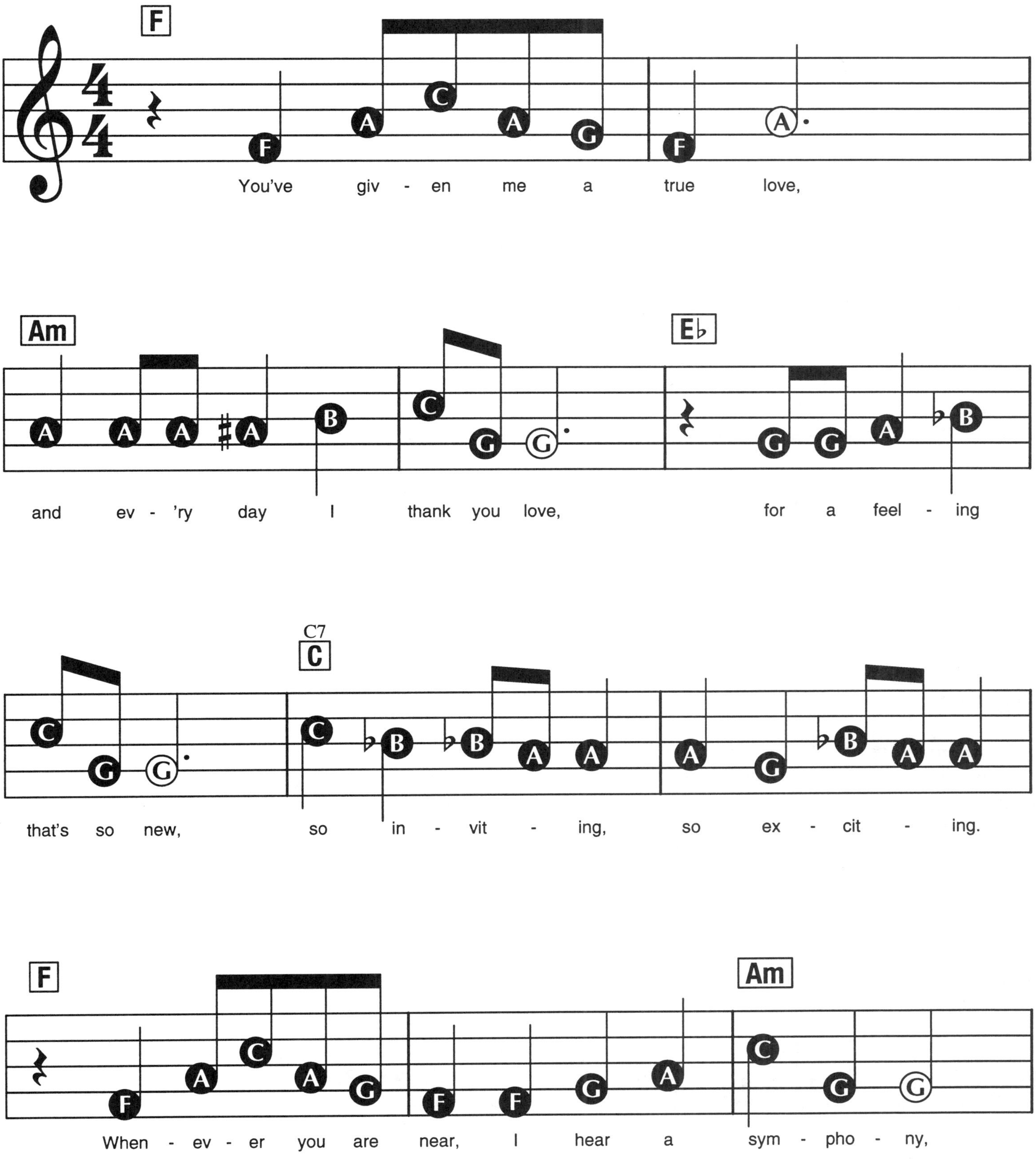

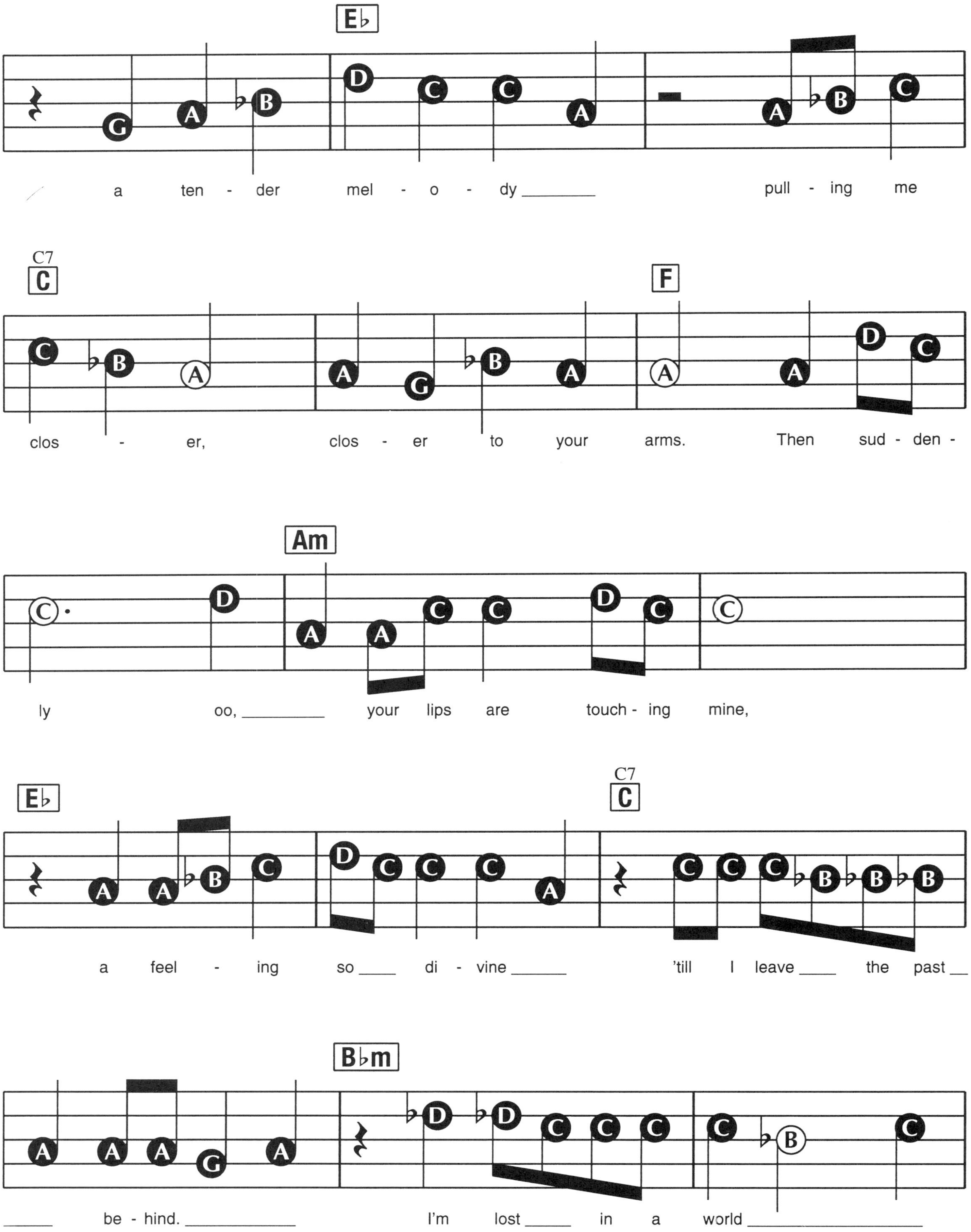
E♭
a ten - der mel - o - dy ____ pull - ing me
C7
C
F
clos - er, clos - er to your arms. Then sud - den -
Am
ly oo, ____ your lips are touch - ing mine,
E♭
C7
C
a feel - ing so ___ di - vine ___ 'till I leave ___ the past __
B♭m
___ be - hind. ______ I'm lost ___ in a world ________

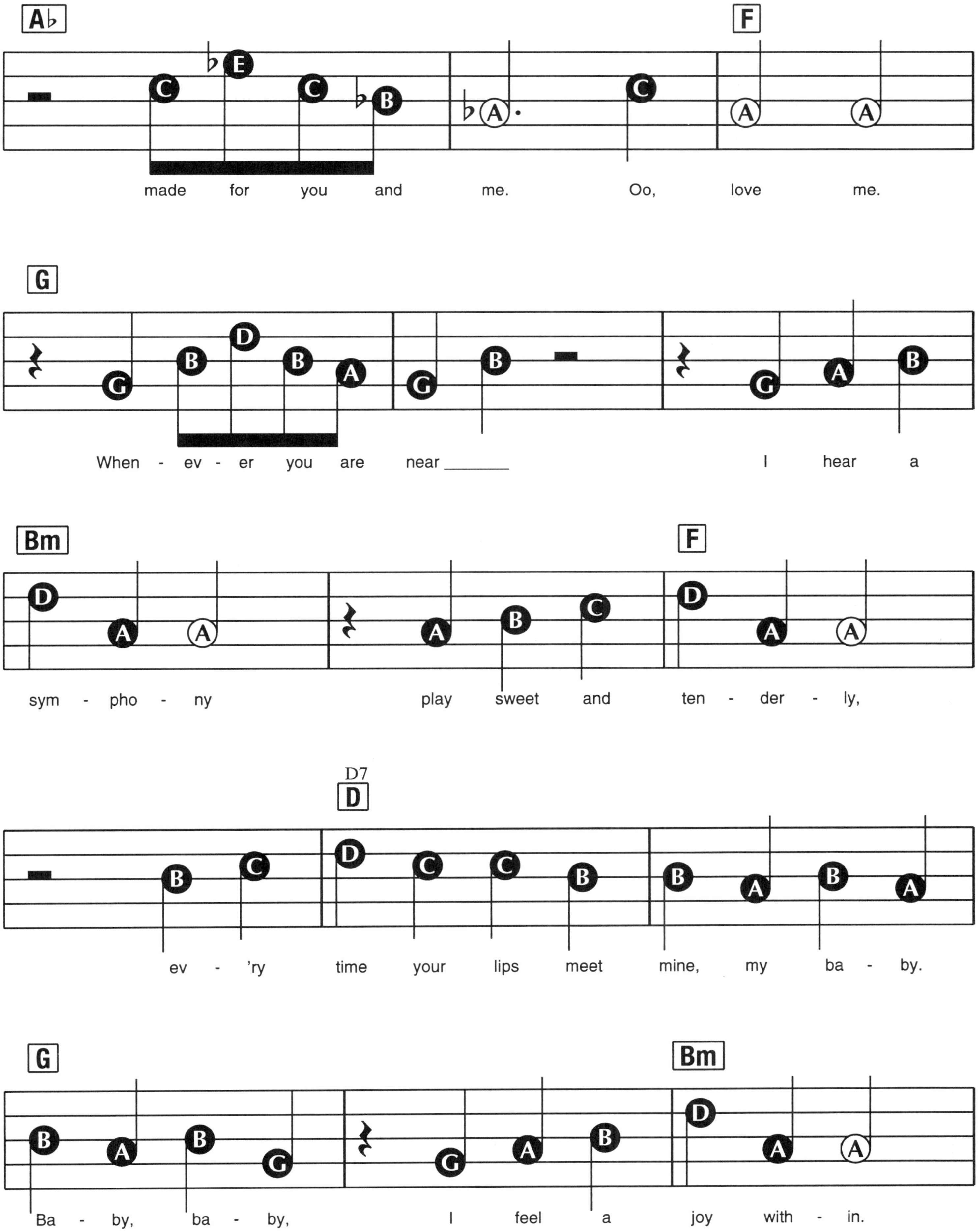
A♭
F
made for you and me. Oo, love me.
G
When - ev - er you are near _______ I hear a
Bm
F
sym - pho - ny play sweet and ten - der - ly,
D7
D
ev - 'ry time your lips meet mine, my ba - by.
G
Bm
Ba - by, ba - by, I feel a joy with - in.

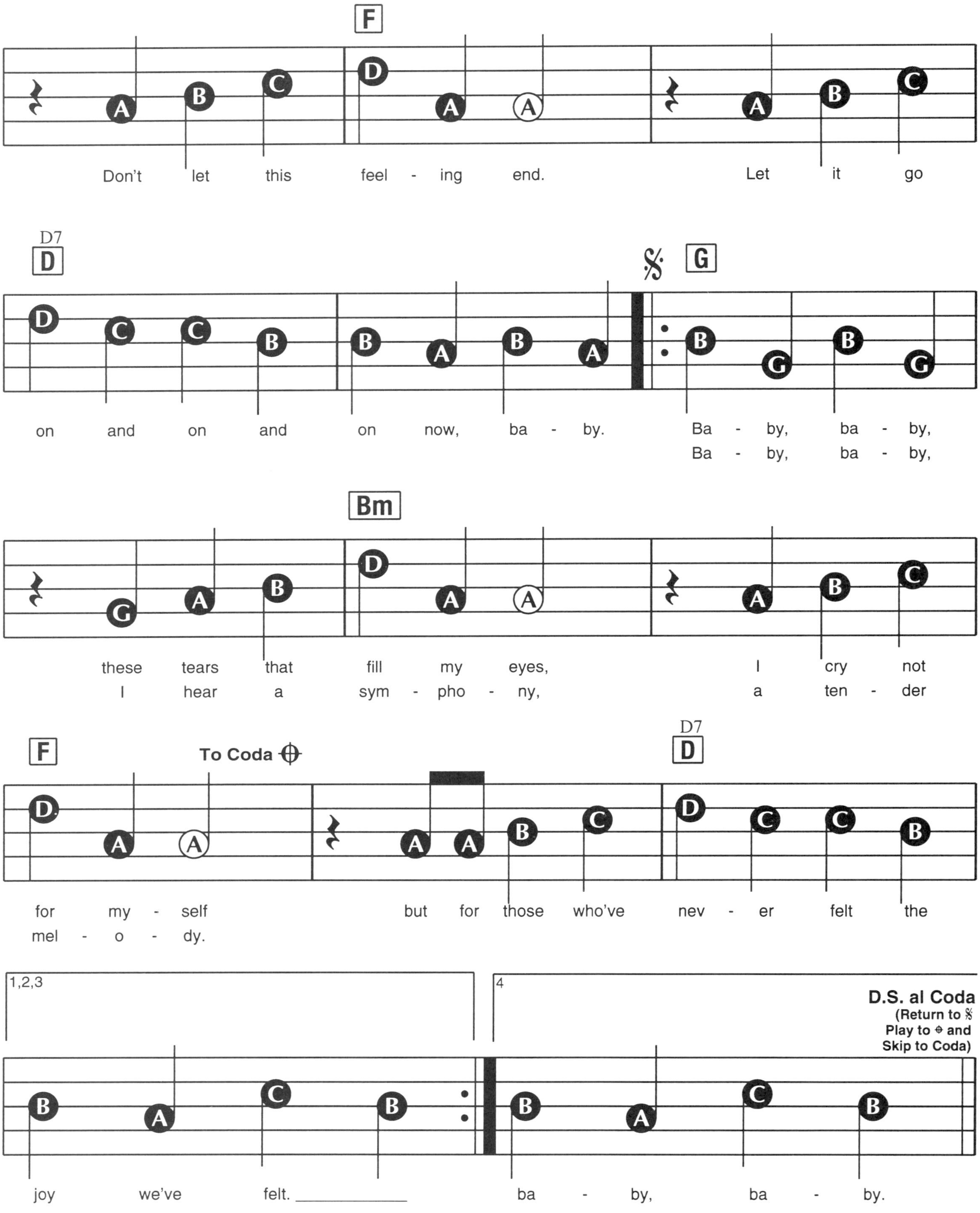
F
Don't let this feel - ing end. Let it go
D7
D
on and on and on now, ba - by.
G
Ba - by, ba - by,
Ba - by, ba - by,
these tears that fill my eyes, I cry not
I hear a sym - pho - ny, a ten - der
Bm
F
To Coda
for my - self but for those who've
mel - o - dy.
D7
D
nev - er felt the
1,2,3
joy we've felt.
4
ba - by, ba - by.
D.S. al Coda
(Return to
Play to and
Skip to Coda)

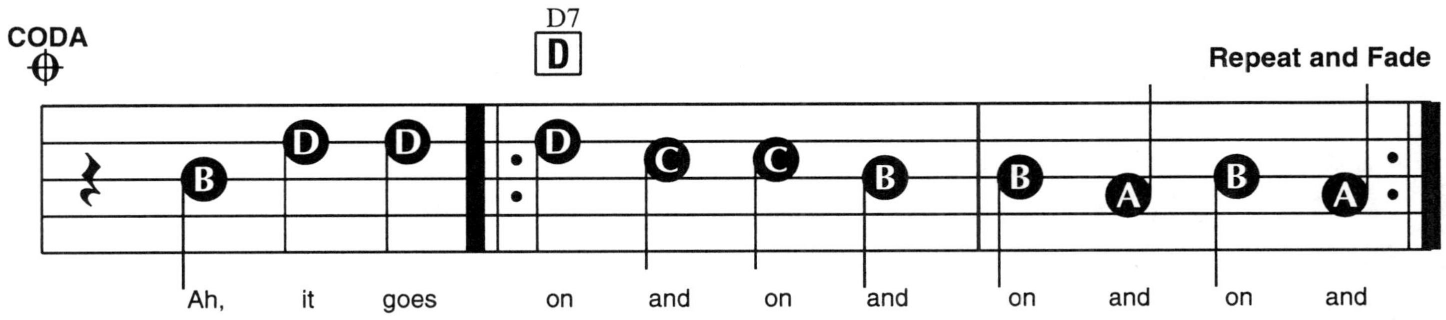

Additional Lyrics

2. Whenever you are near
   I hear a symphony,
   each time you speak to me
   I hear a tender rhapsody of love, love.

3. Baby, baby,
   as you stand up holding me
   whispering how much you care
   a thousand violins fill the air now.

4. Baby, baby,
   don't let this moment end.
   Keep standing close to me,
   oo so close to me, baby, baby.

I Heard It Through the Grapevine

Registration 2
Rhythm: Rock or Disco

Words and Music by Norman Whitfield
and Barrett Strong

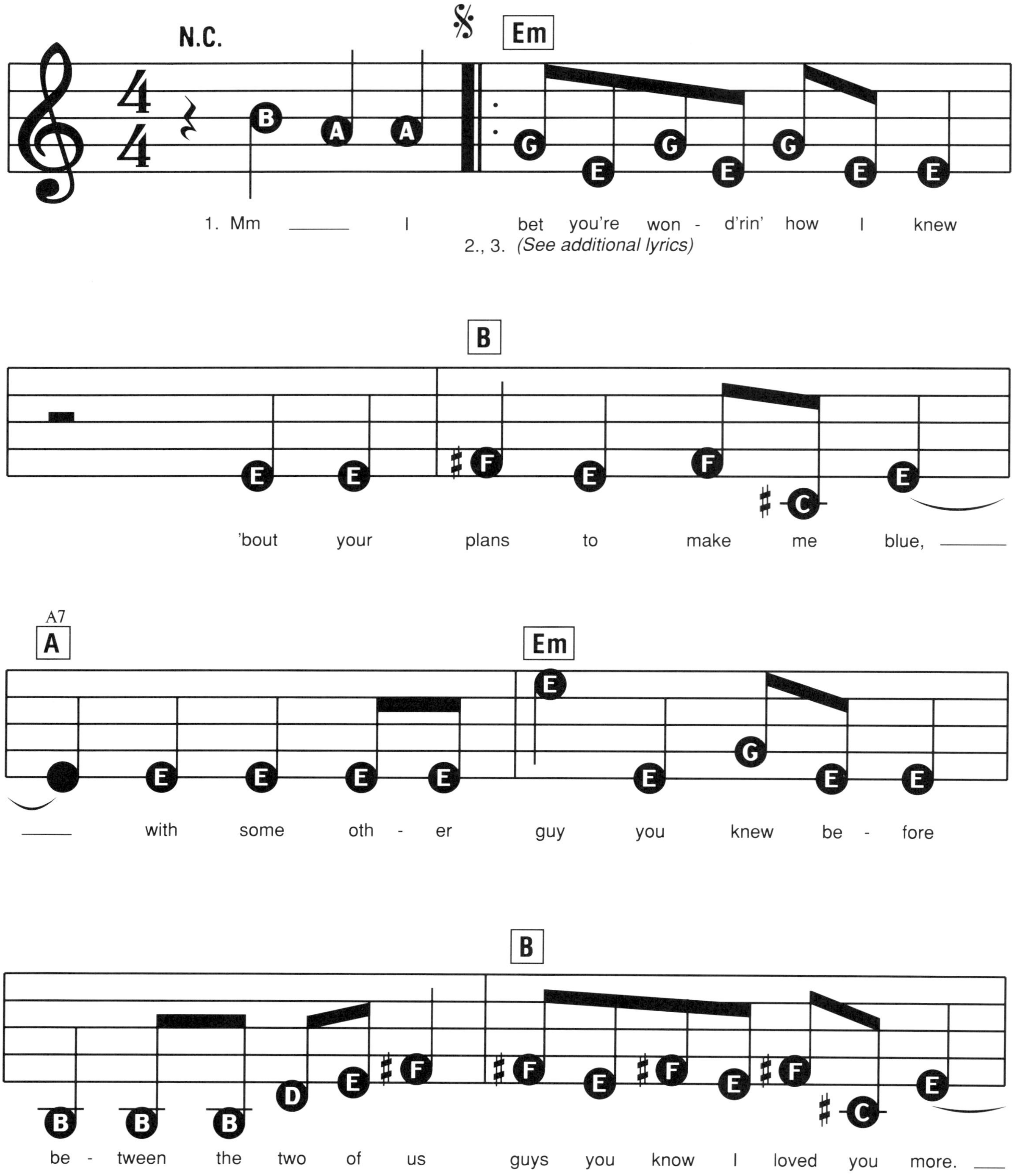

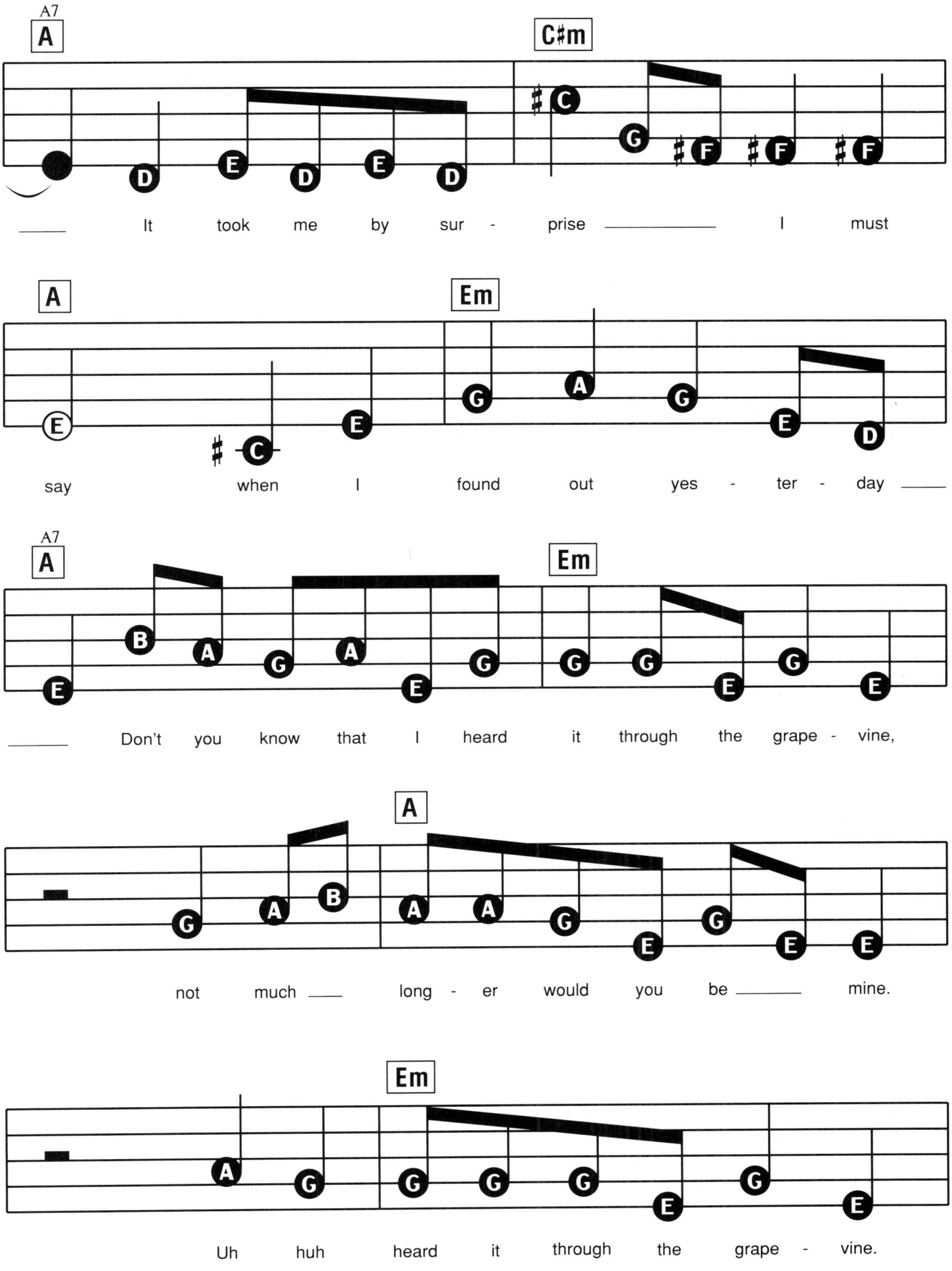
A7
A
C♯m
It took me by sur - prise I must
A
Em
say when I found out yes - ter - day
A7
A
Em
Don't you know that I heard it through the grape - vine,
A
not much long - er would you be mine.
Em
Uh huh heard it through the grape - vine.

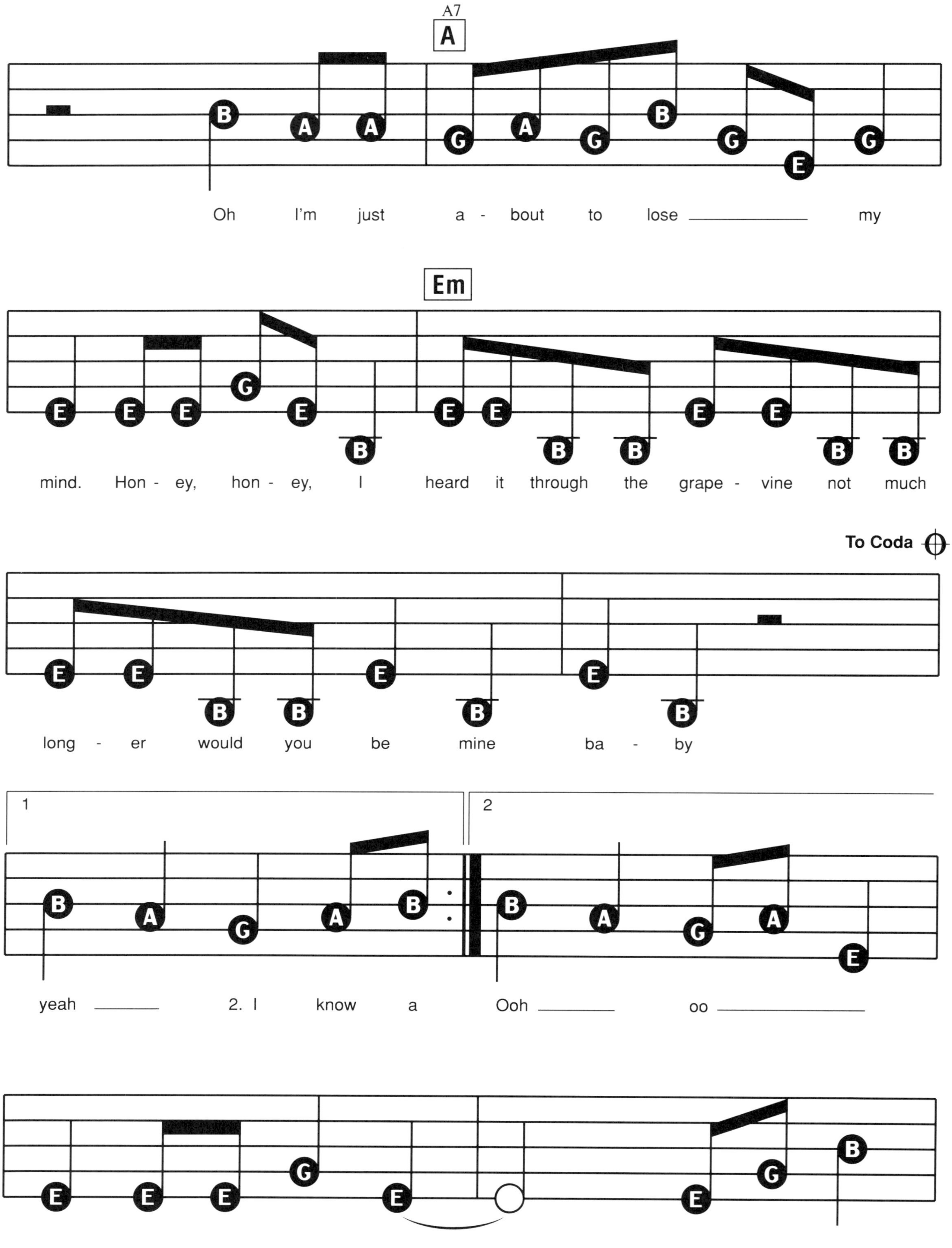
A7
A
Oh I'm just a - bout to lose my
Em
mind. Hon - ey, hon - ey, I heard it through the grape - vine not much
To Coda
long - er would you be mine ba - by
1
yeah 2. I know a
2
Ooh oo

Additional Lyrics

2. I know a man ain't supposed to cry
But these tears I can't hold inside,
Losin' you would end my life you see
'Cause you mean that much to me.
You could have told me yourself
That you loved someone else.
Instead, I heard it through the grapevine,
Not much longer would you be mine.
Oh, I heard it through the grapevine,
And I'm just about to lose my mind.

3. People say believe half of what you see
Oh, and none of what you hear;
But I can't help but be confused.
If it's true please tell me dear.
Do you plan to let me go
For the other guy you loved before?

I Second That Emotion

Registration 9
Rhythm: Rock or 16-Beat

Words and Music by William "Smokey" Robinson
and Alfred Cleveland

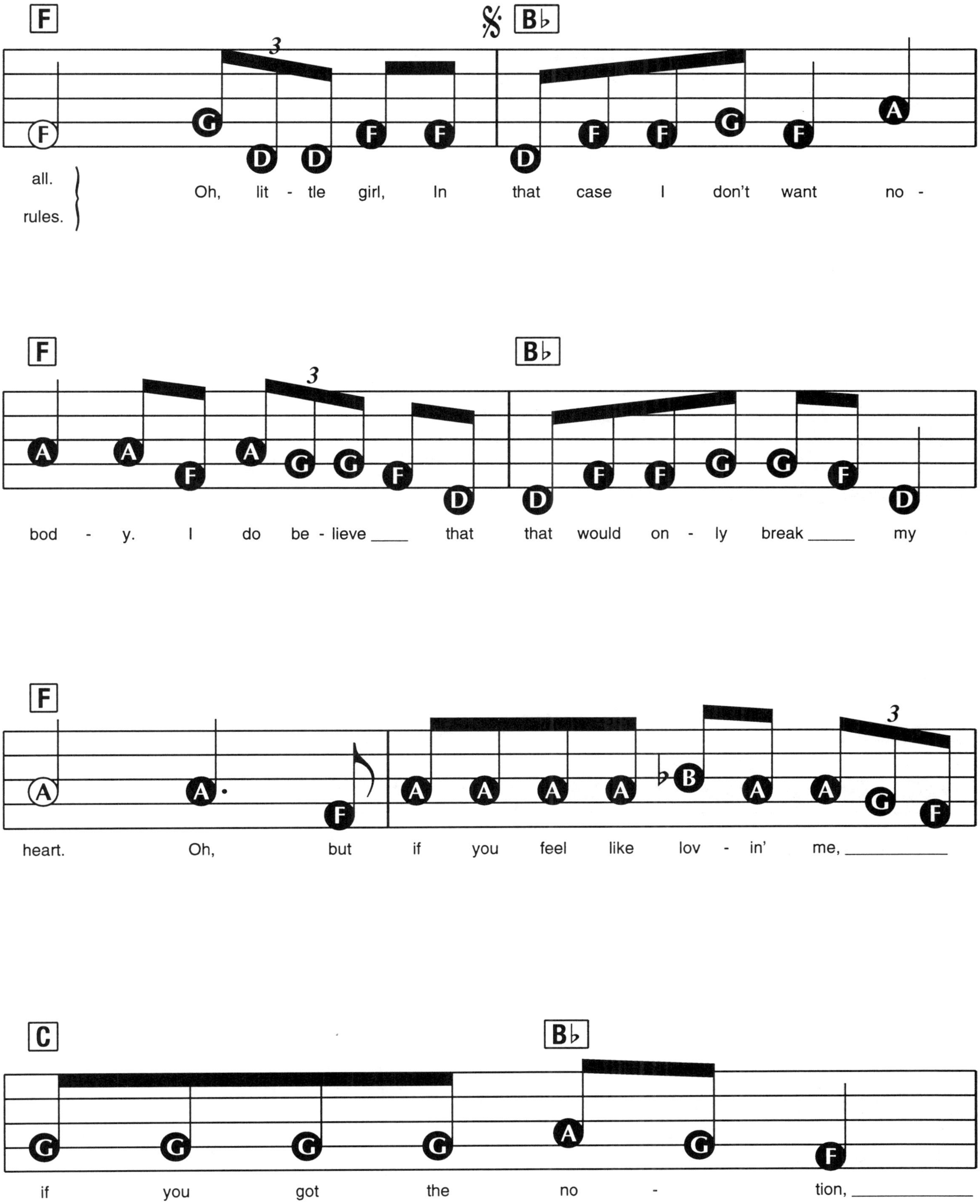
F
B♭
all.
rules.
Oh, lit - tle girl, In that case I don't want no -
F
B♭
bod - y. I do be - lieve ____ that that would on - ly break _____ my
F
heart. Oh, but if you feel like lov - in' me, ___________
C
B♭
if you got the no - tion, ___________

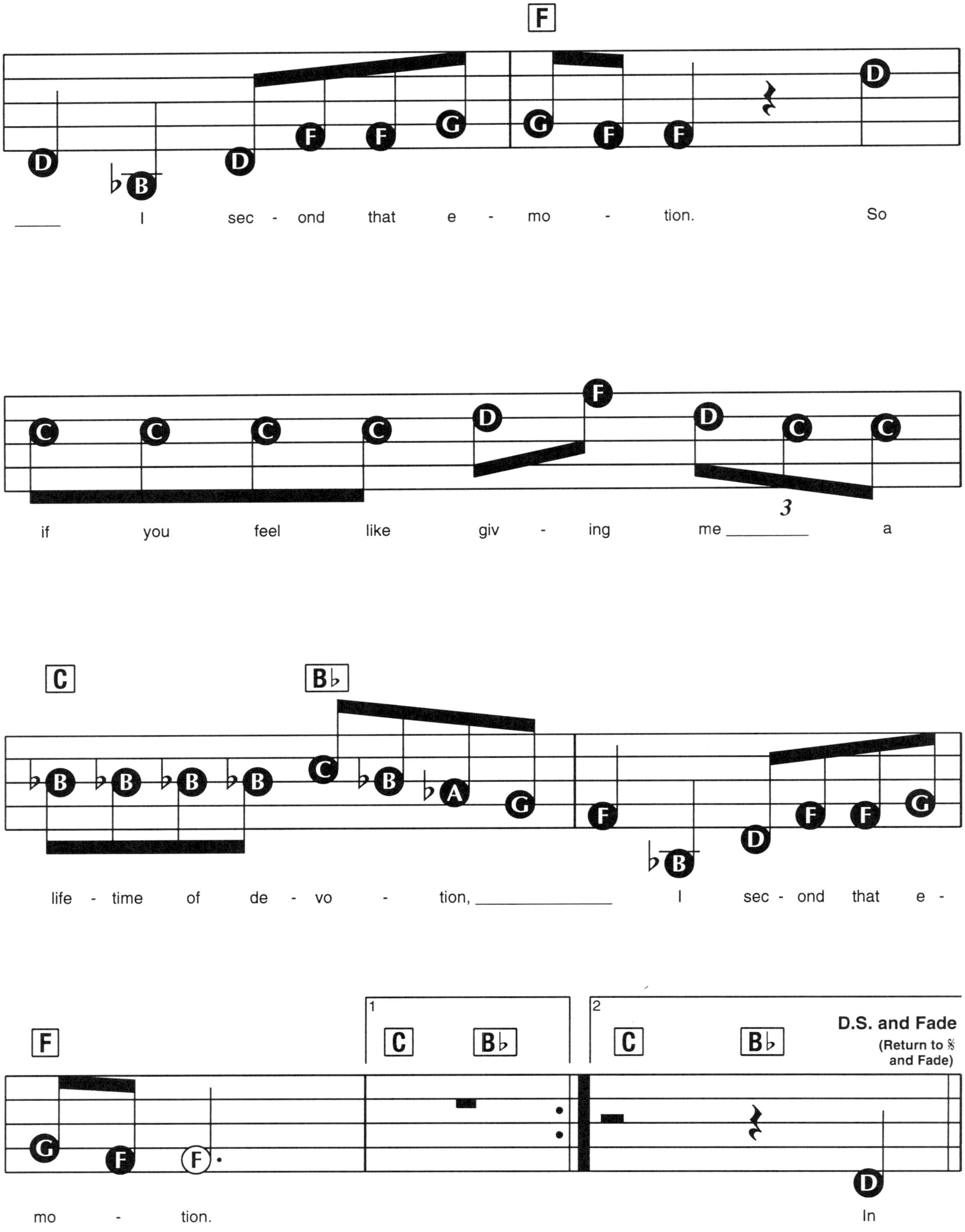
F
I sec - ond that e - mo - tion. So
if you feel like giv - ing me a
3
C
B♭
life - time of de - vo - tion, I sec - ond that e -
F
mo - tion.
1
C
B♭
2
C
B♭
D.S. and Fade
(Return to 𝄋 and Fade)
In

Let's Get It On

Registration 7
Rhythm: Rock or 8 Beat

Words and Music by Marvin Gaye
and Ed Townsend

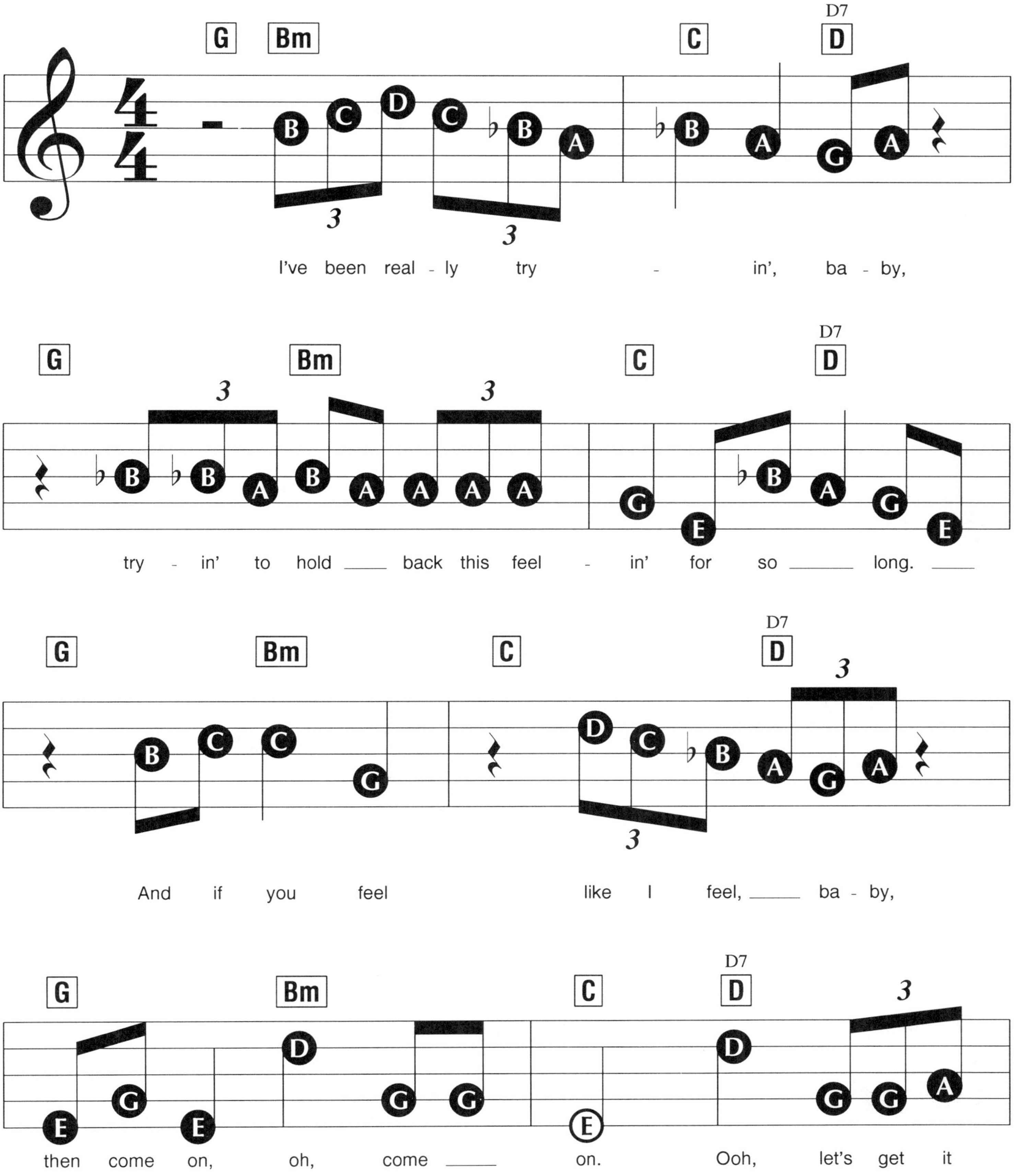

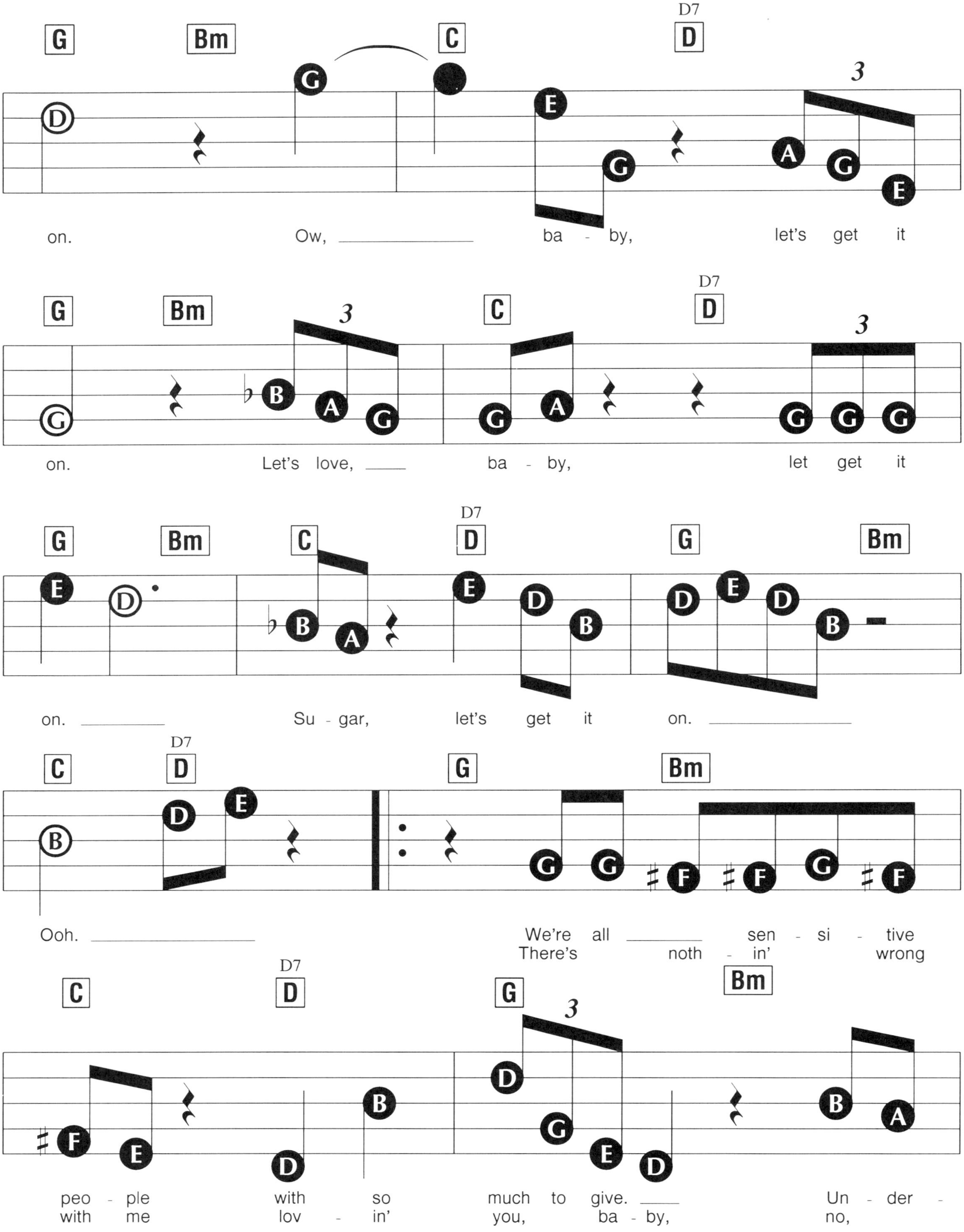
on. Ow, ___ ba - by, let's get it
on. Let's love, ___ ba - by, let get it
on. ___ Su - gar, let's get it on. ___
Ooh. ___ We're all ___ sen - si - tive
There's noth - in' wrong
peo - ple with so much to give. ___ Un - der -
with me lov - in' you, ba - by, no,

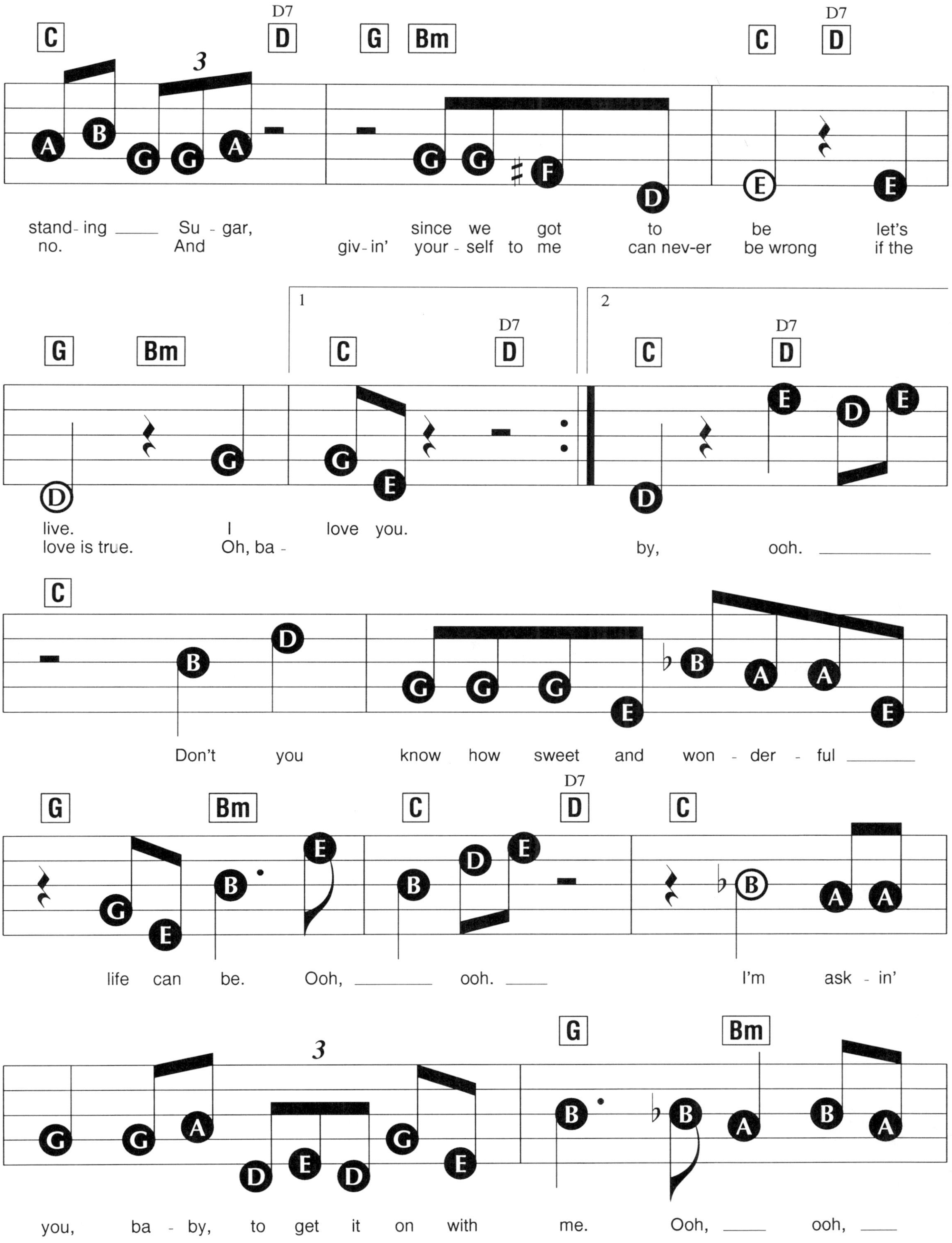
C D7 D G Bm C D7 D
stand - ing ____ Su - gar, since we got to be let's
no. And giv - in' your - self to me can nev-er be wrong if the
G Bm 1 C D7 D 2 C D7 D
live. I love you.
love is true. Oh, ba - by, ooh. ____
C
Don't you know how sweet and won - der - ful ____
G Bm C D7 D C
life can be. Ooh, ____ ooh. ____ I'm ask - in'
G Bm
you, ba - by, to get it on with me. Ooh, ____ ooh, ____

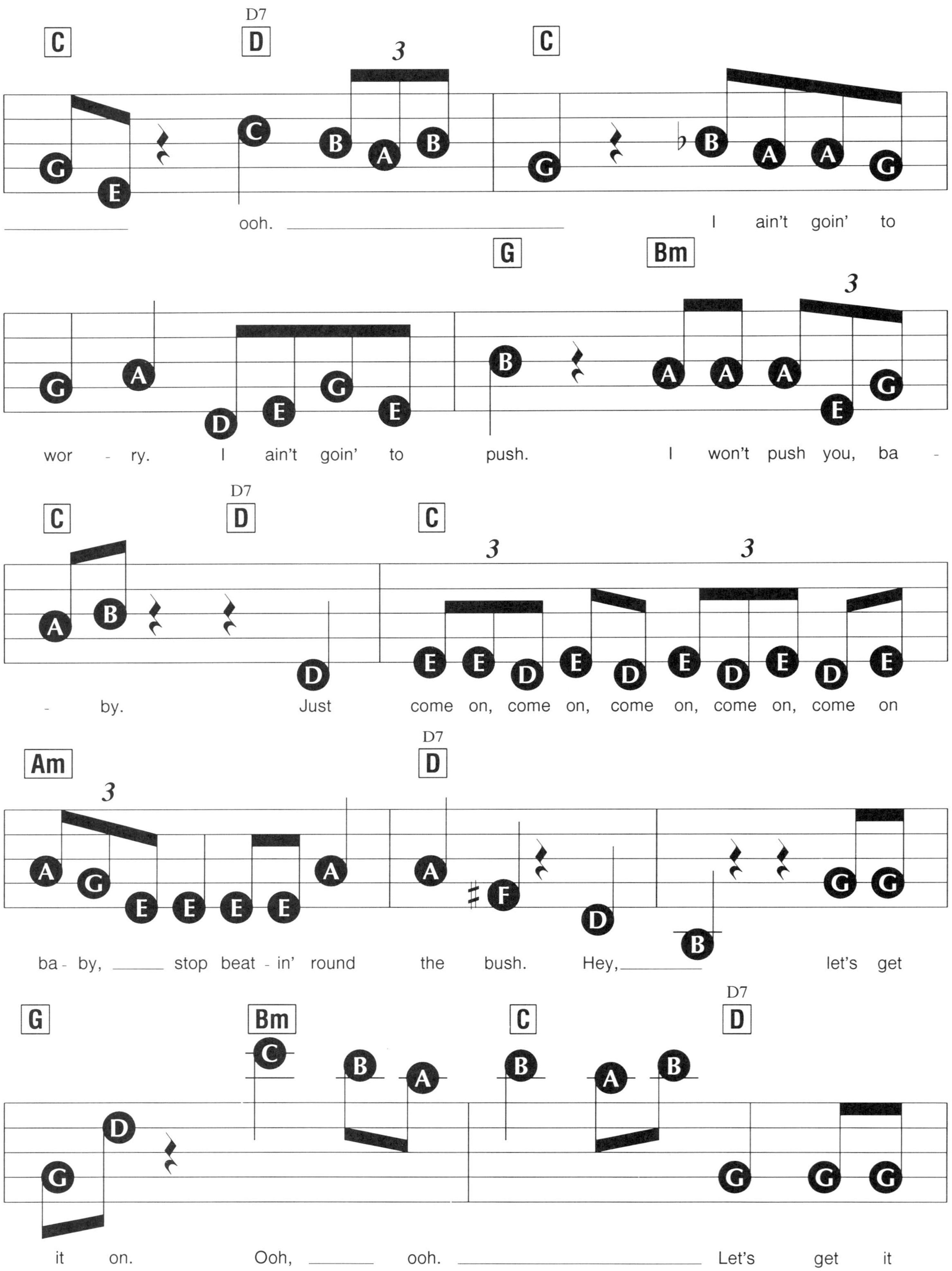
C D7 D C
ooh. I ain't goin' to
G Bm
wor - ry. I ain't goin' to push. I won't push you, ba -
C D7 D C
- by. Just come on, come on, come on, come on, come on
Am D7 D
ba - by, stop beat - in' round the bush. Hey, let's get
G Bm C D7 D
it on. Ooh, ooh. Let's get it

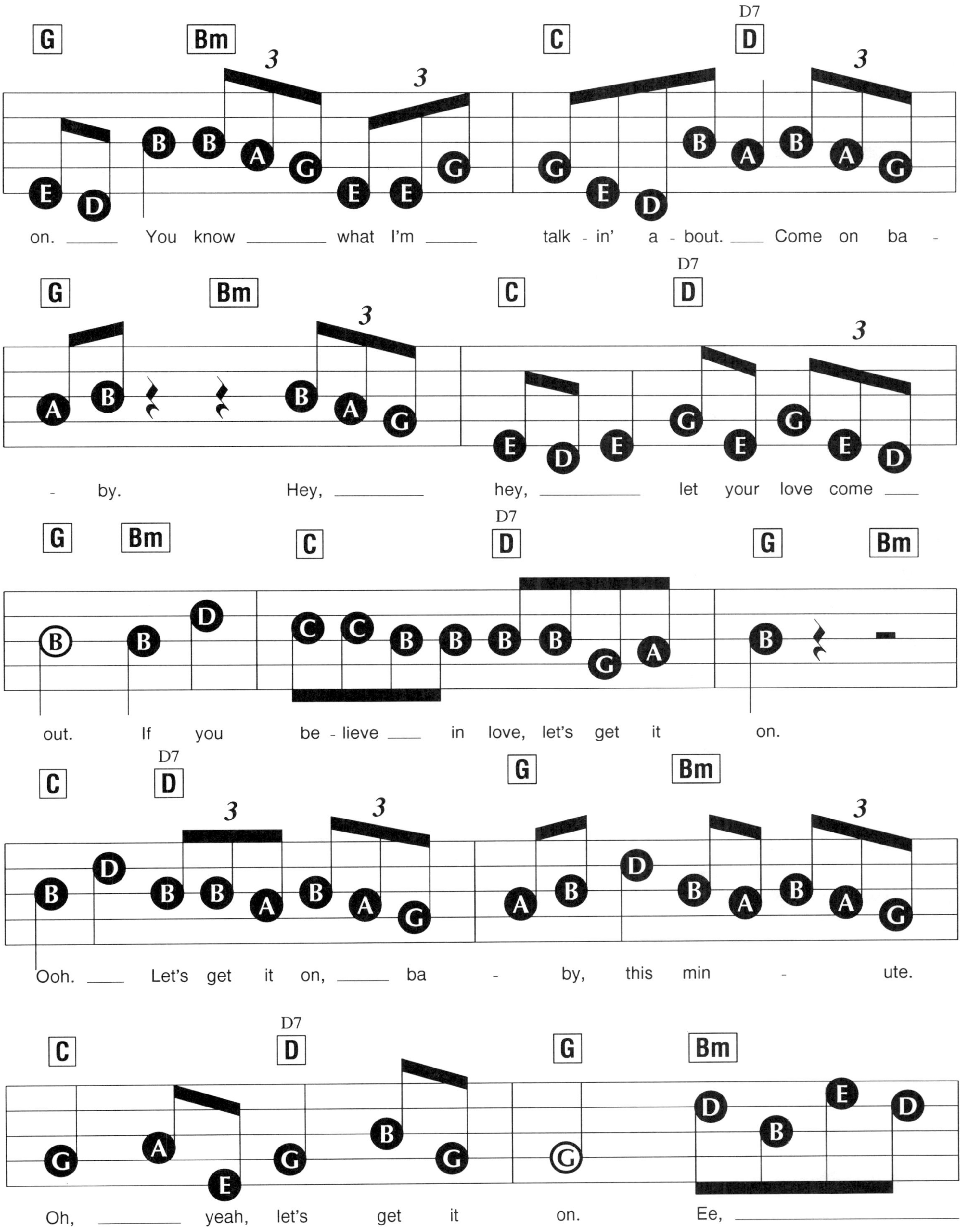
G Bm C D7 D
on. You know what I'm talk - in' a - bout. Come on ba -
G Bm C D7 D
- by. Hey, hey, let your love come
G Bm C D7 D G Bm
out. If you be - lieve in love, let's get it on.
C D7 D G Bm
Ooh. Let's get it on, ba - by, this min - ute.
C D7 D G Bm
Oh, yeah, let's get it on. Ee,

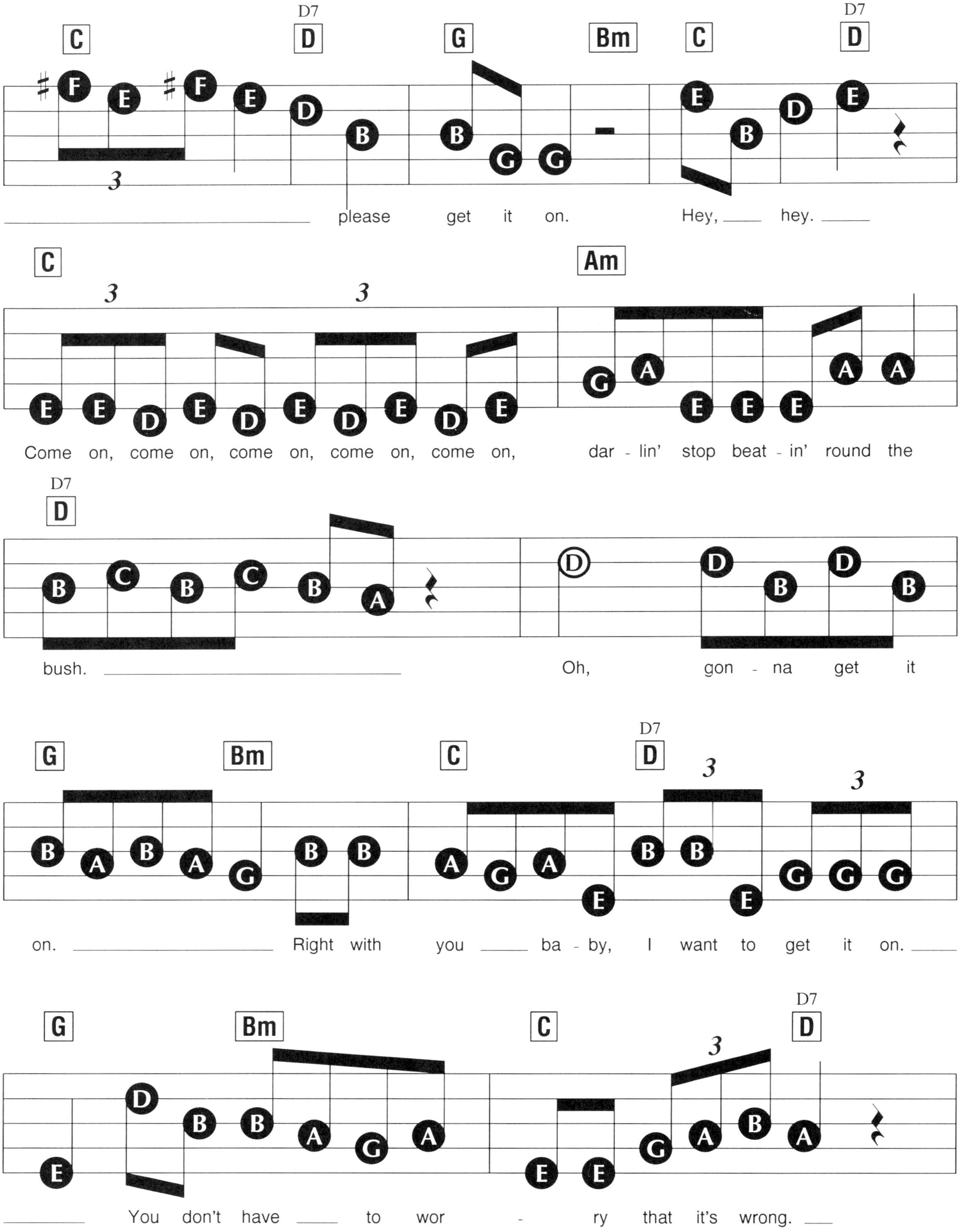
C D7 D G Bm C D7 D
please get it on. Hey, hey.
C Am
Come on, come on, come on, come on, come on, dar - lin' stop beat - in' round the
D7 D
bush. Oh, gon - na get it
G Bm C D7 D
on. Right with you ba - by, I want to get it on.
G Bm C D7 D
You don't have to wor - ry that it's wrong.

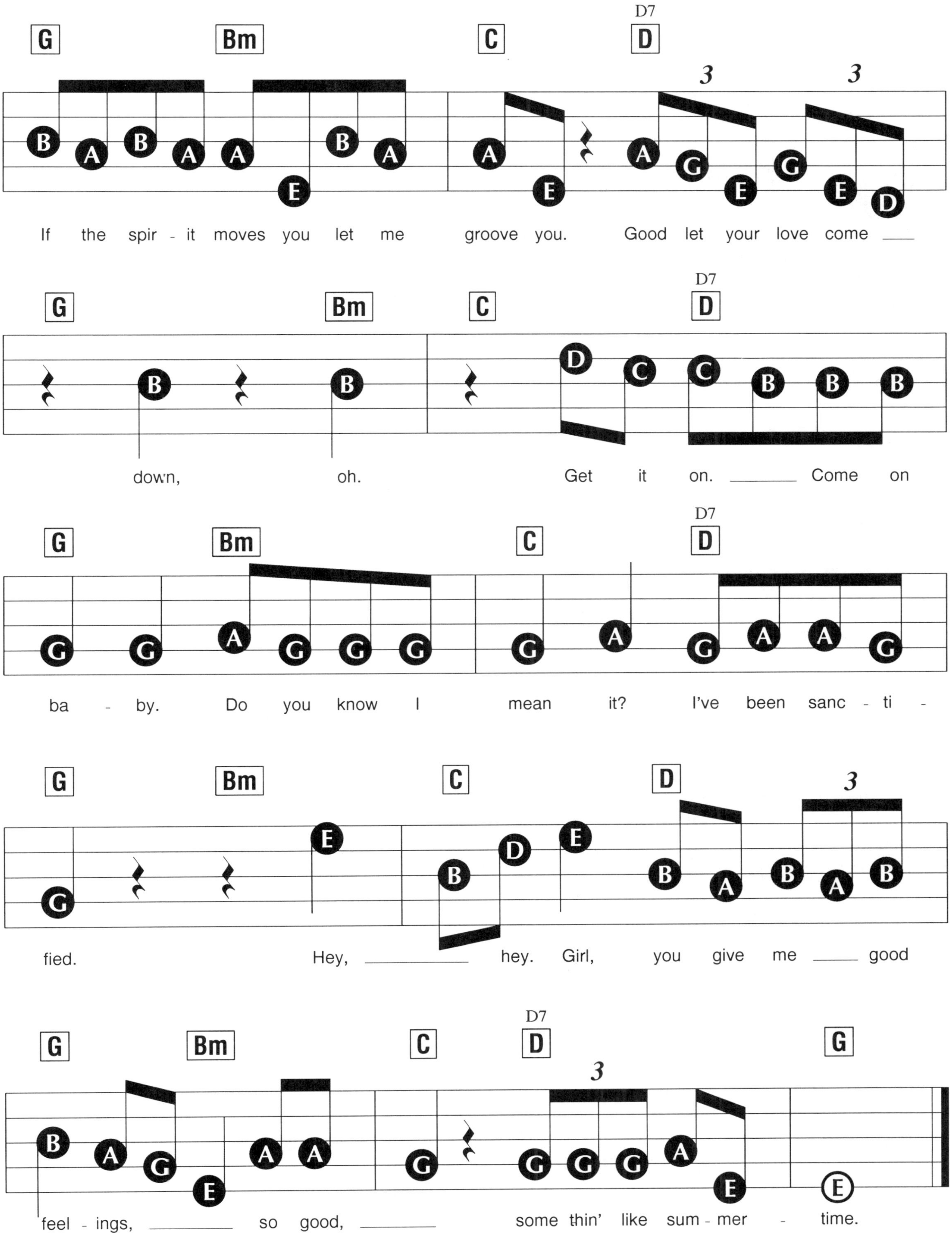
G Bm C D7 D
If the spir - it moves you let me groove you. Good let your love come
G Bm C D7 D
down, oh. Get it on. Come on
G Bm C D7 D
ba - by. Do you know I mean it? I've been sanc - ti -
G Bm C D
fied. Hey, hey. Girl, you give me good
G Bm C D7 D G
feel - ings, so good, some thin' like sum - mer - time.

I'll Be There

Registration 9
Rhythm: Rock or 8-Beat

Words and Music by Berry Gordy, Hal Davis,
Willie Hutch and Bob West

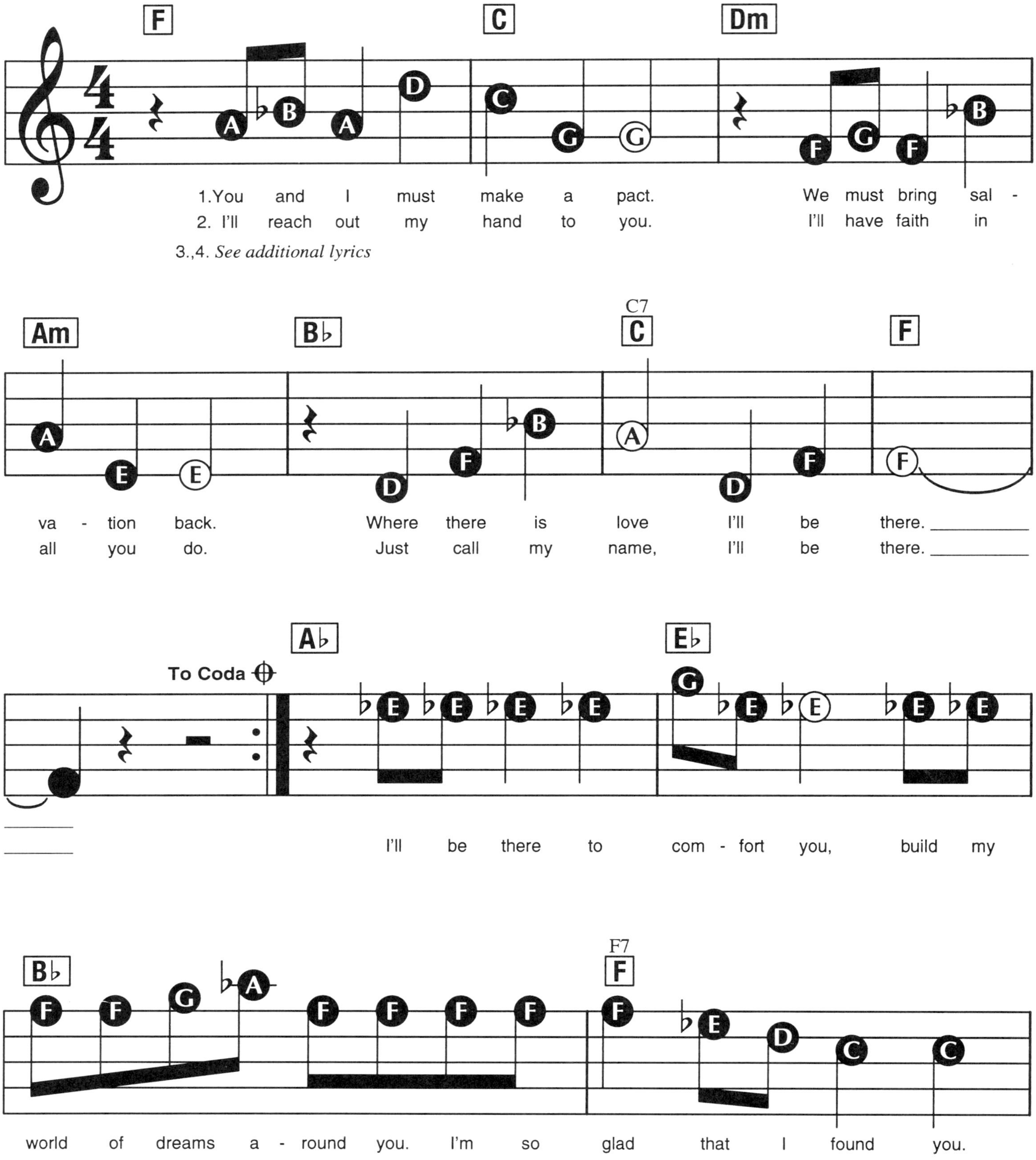

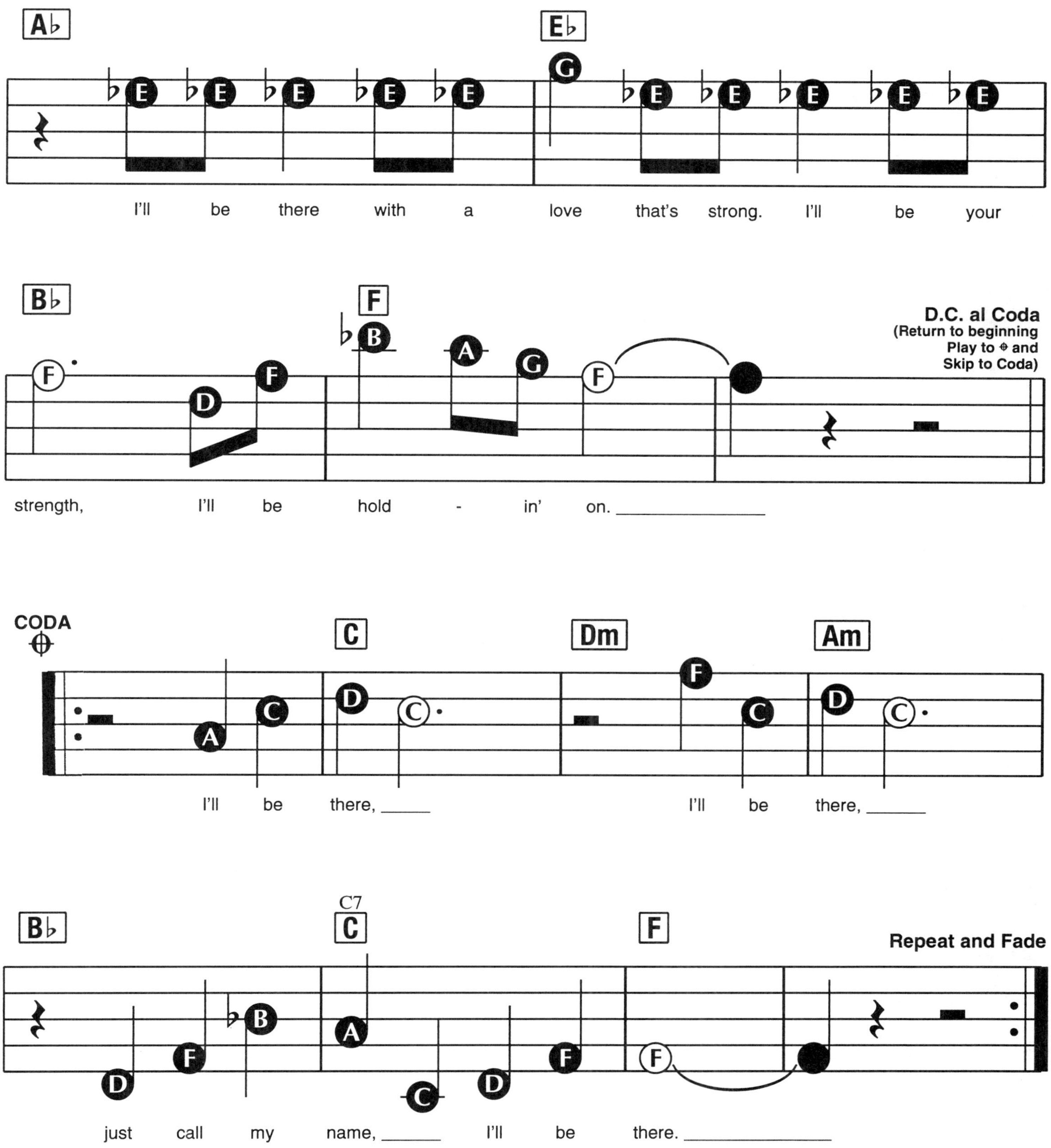

Additional Lyrics

3. Let me fill your heart with joy and laughter.
   Togetherness, girl, is all I'm after.
   Whenever you need me, I'll be there.

4. I'll be there to protect you
   With unselfish love that respects you.
   Just call my name, I'll be there.

Just My Imagination
(Running Away with Me)

Registration 3
Rhythm: Rock or 8-Beat

Words and Music by Norman Whitfield
and Barrett Strong

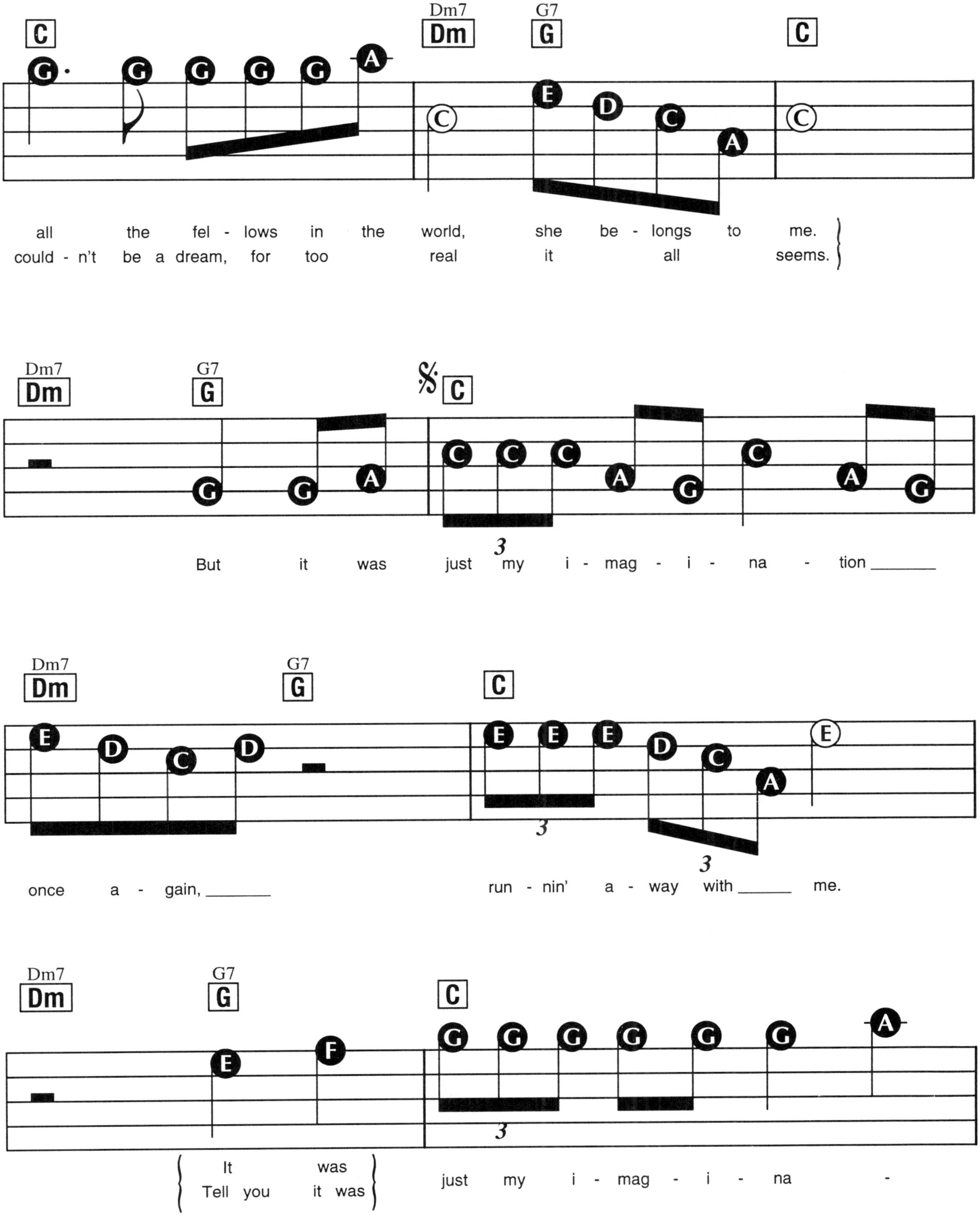
C
Dm7 Dm
G7 G
C
all the fel - lows in the world, she be - longs to me.
could - n't be a dream, for too real it all seems.
Dm7 Dm
G7 G
C
But it was just my i - mag - i - na - tion
Dm7 Dm
G7 G
C
once a - gain,
run - nin' a - way with me.
Dm7 Dm
G7 G
C
It was
Tell you it was
just my i - mag - i - na -

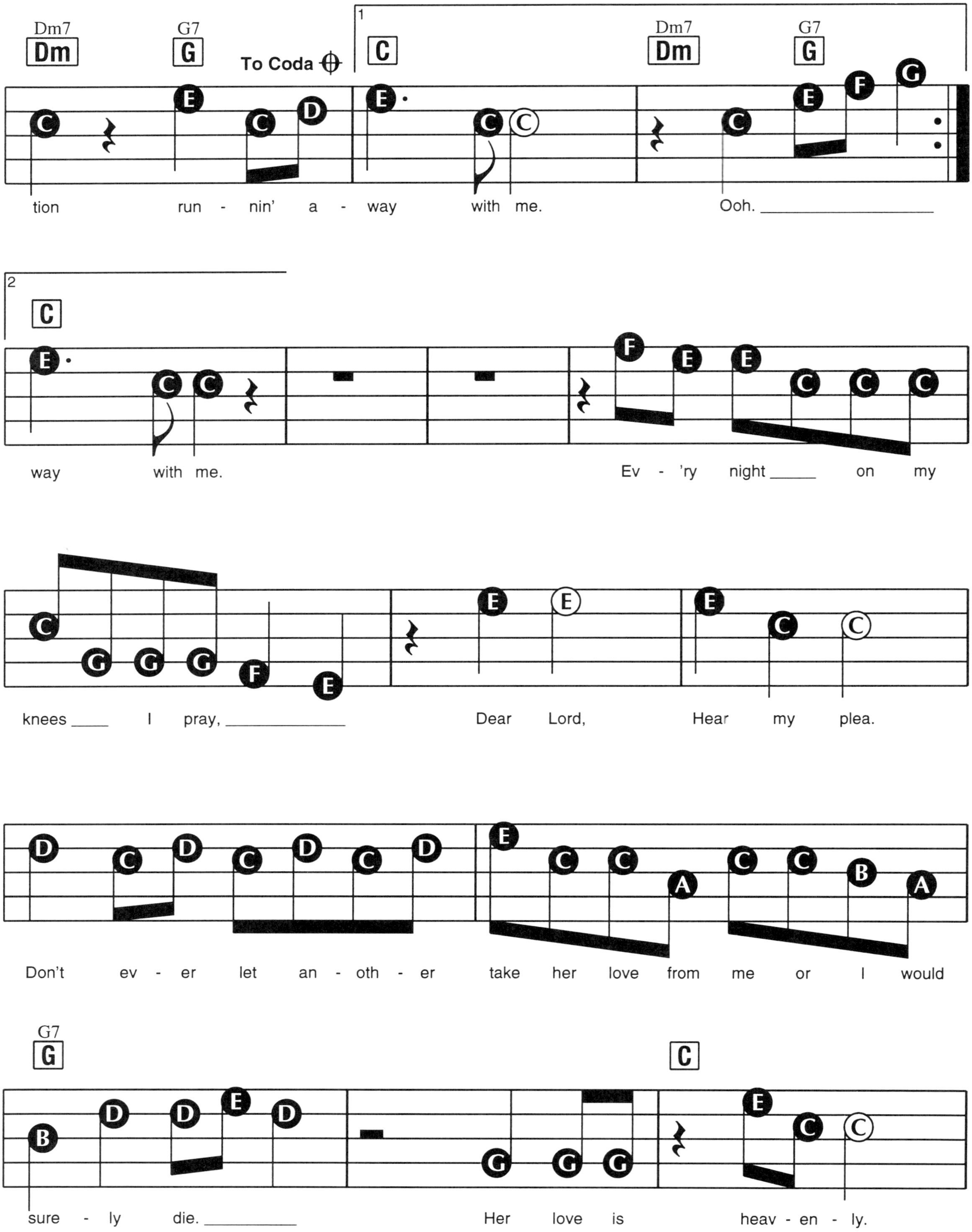
Dm7 Dm G7 G To Coda
1 C Dm7 Dm G7 G
tion run - nin' a - way with me. Ooh.
2 C
way with me. Ev - 'ry night on my
knees I pray, Dear Lord, Hear my plea.
Don't ev - er let an - oth - er take her love from me or I would
G7 G C
sure - ly die. Her love is heav - en - ly.

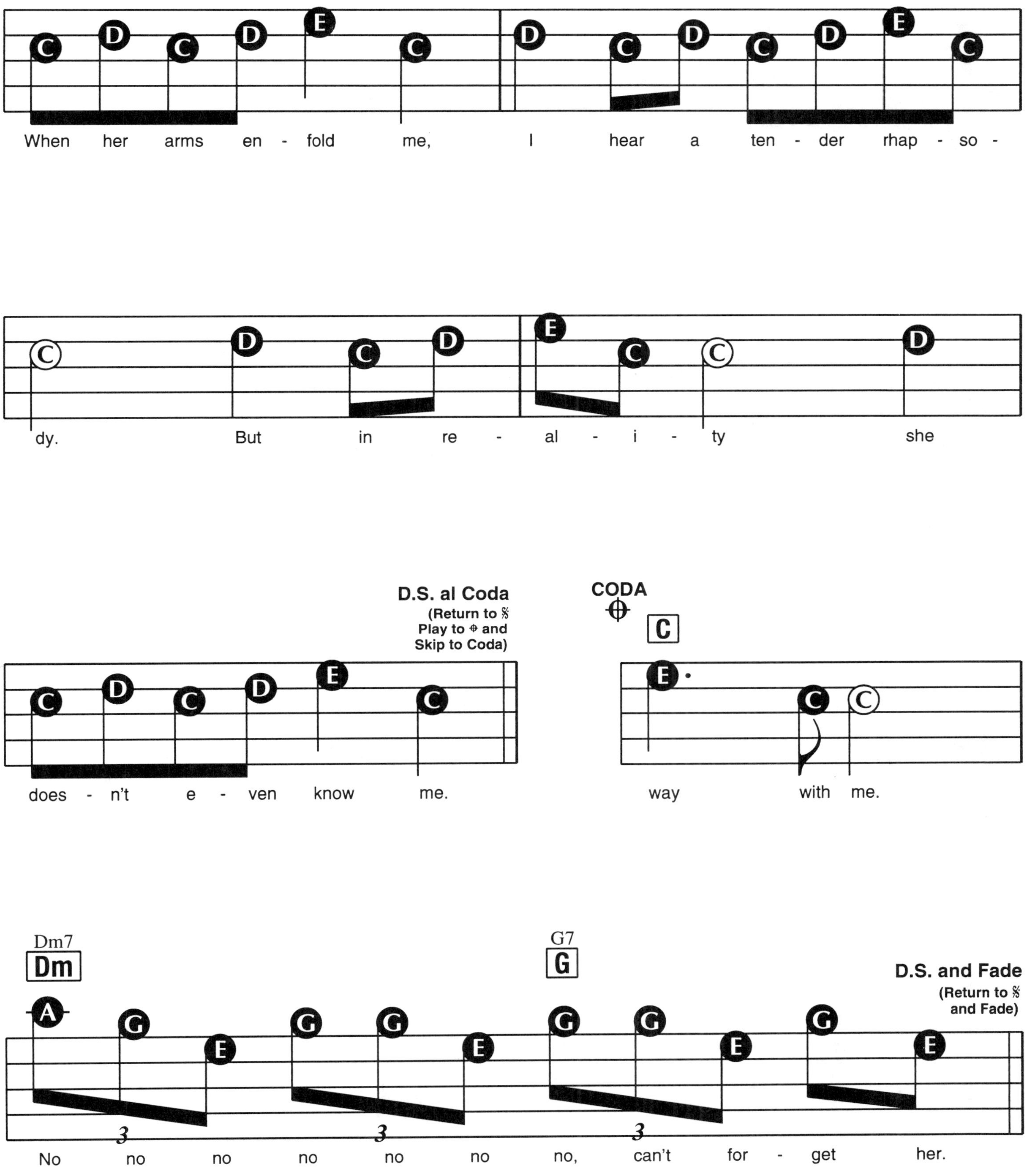
When her arms en - fold me, I hear a ten - der rhap - so -
dy. But in re - al - i - ty she
D.S. al Coda
(Return to 𝄋 Play to ⊕ and Skip to Coda)
does - n't e - ven know me.
CODA
C
way with me.
Dm7
Dm
G7
G
D.S. and Fade
(Return to 𝄋 and Fade)
No no no no no no no, can't for - get her.

Maybe Tomorrow

Registration 3
Rhythm: Rock or 8 Beat

Words and Music by Berry Gordy, Alphonso J. Mizell,
Frederick J. Perren and Deke Richards

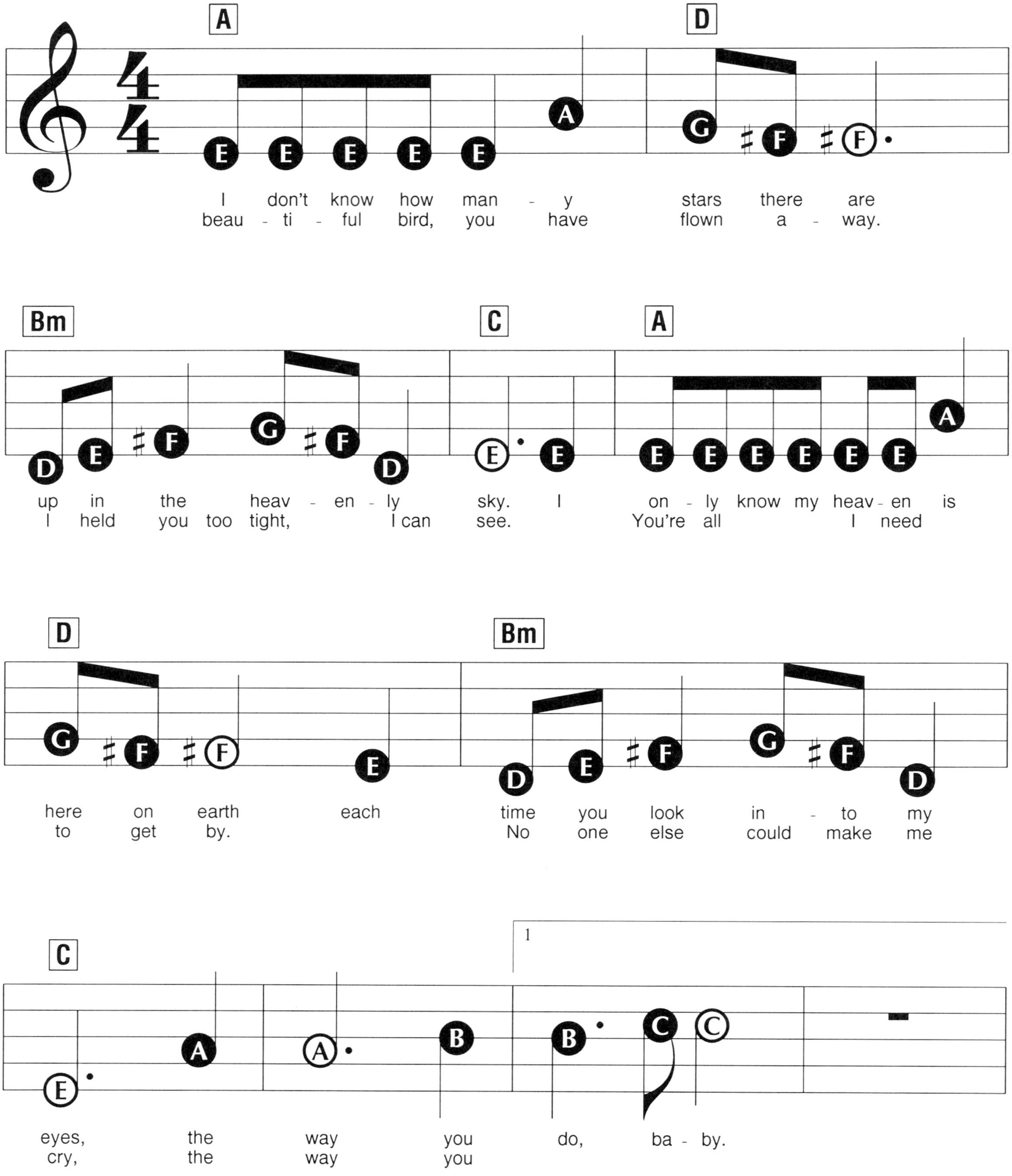

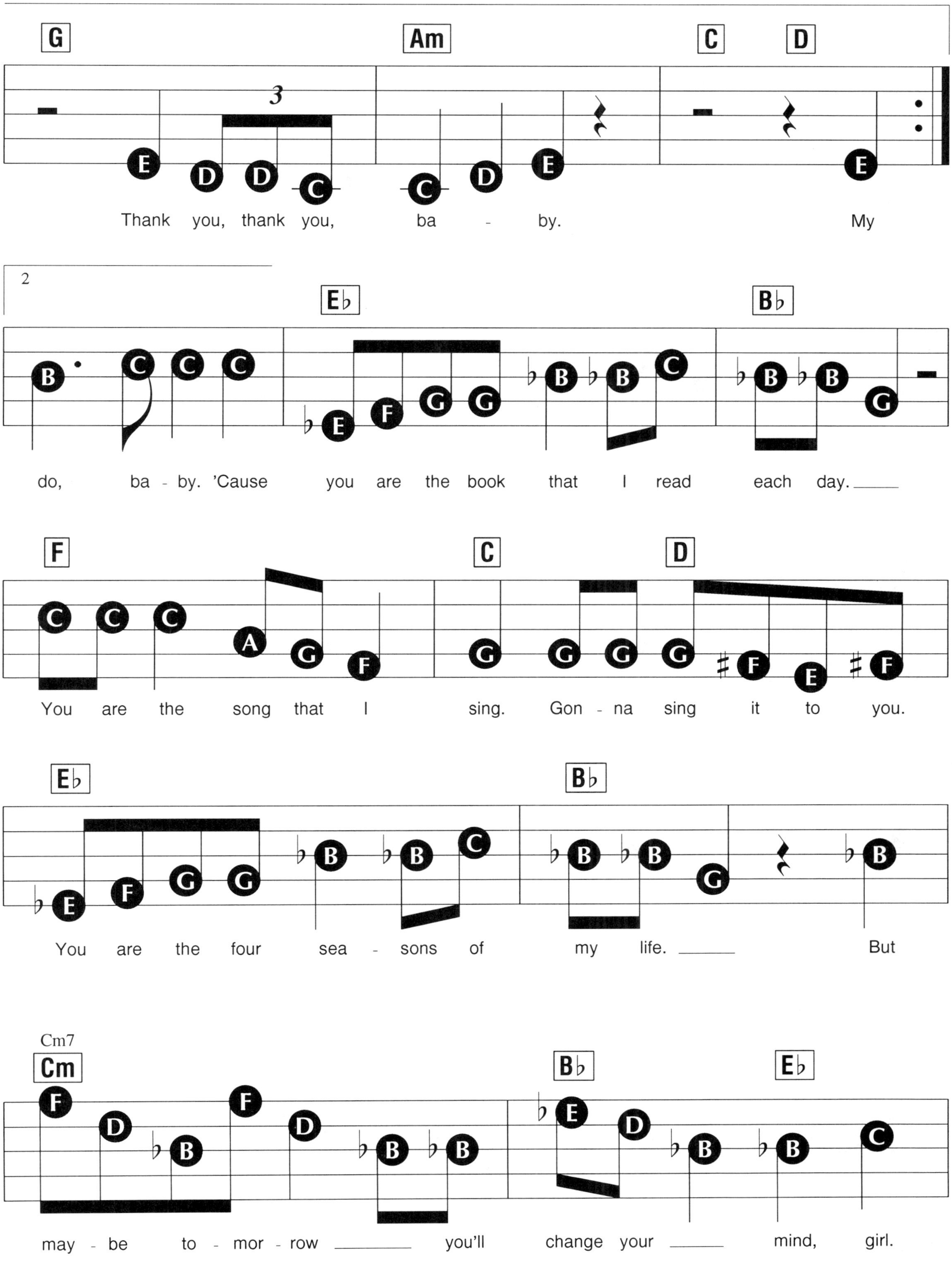
G
Am
C
D
3
Thank you, thank you, ba - by. My
2
E♭
B♭
do, ba - by. 'Cause you are the book that I read each day.
F
C
D
You are the song that I sing. Gon - na sing it to you.
E♭
B♭
You are the four sea - sons of my life. But
Cm7
Cm
B♭
E♭
may - be to - mor - row you'll change your mind, girl.

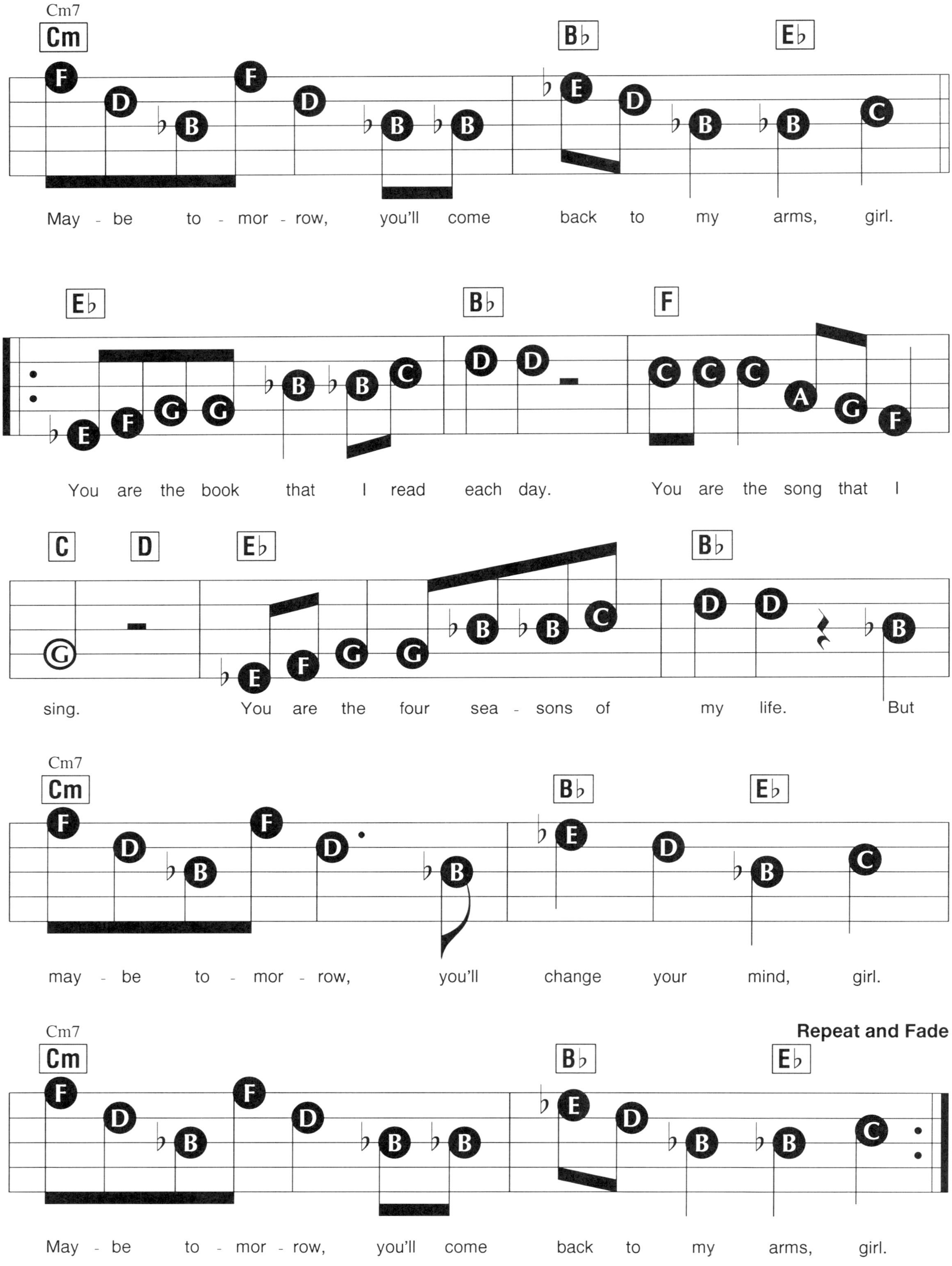
Cm7
Cm
B♭
E♭
May - be to - mor - row, you'll come back to my arms, girl.
E♭
B♭
F
You are the book that I read each day. You are the song that I
C
D
E♭
B♭
sing. You are the four sea - sons of my life. But
Cm7
Cm
B♭
E♭
may - be to - mor - row, you'll change your mind, girl.
Cm7
Cm
B♭
E♭
Repeat and Fade
May - be to - mor - row, you'll come back to my arms, girl.

Mercy, Mercy Me
(The Ecology)

Registration 1
Rhythm: Rock or 16-Beat

Words and Music by
Marvin Gaye

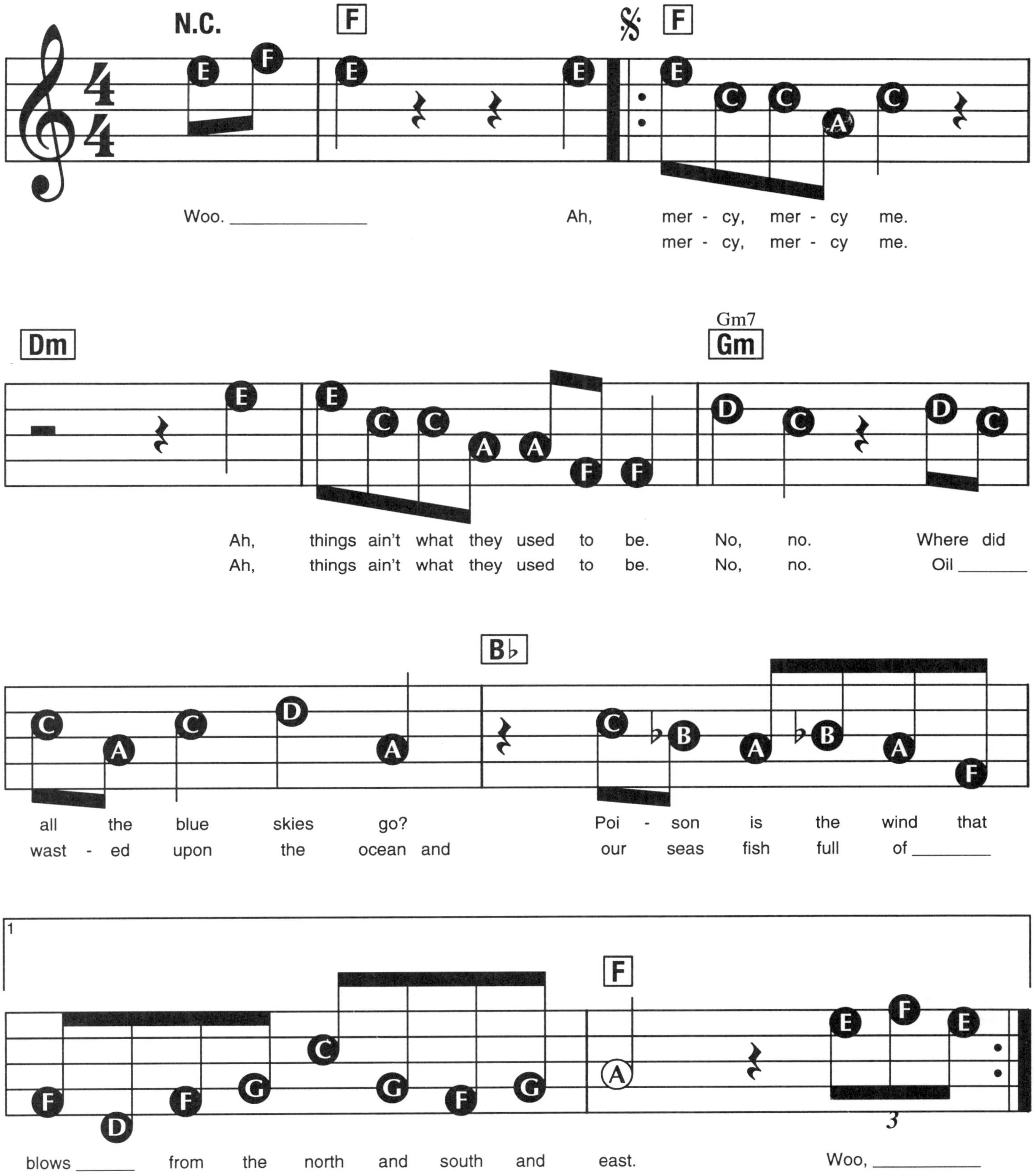

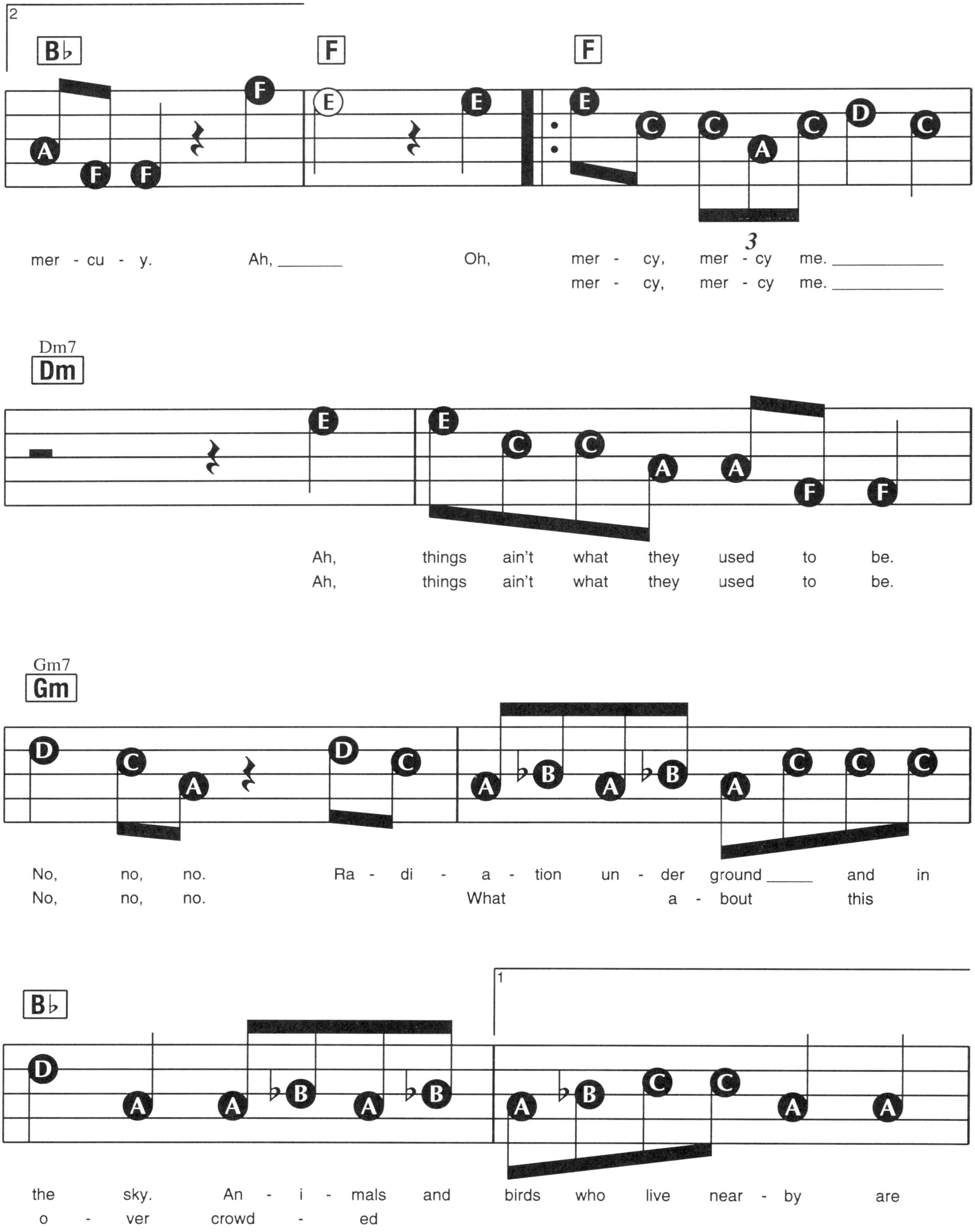
B♭
F
F
mer - cu - y. Ah, Oh, mer - cy, mer - cy me.
mer - cy, mer - cy me.
3
Dm7
Dm
Ah, things ain't what they used to be.
Ah, things ain't what they used to be.
Gm7
Gm
No, no, no. Ra - di - a - tion un - der ground and in
No, no, no. What a - bout this
B♭
the sky. An - i - mals and birds who live near - by are
o - ver crowd - ed

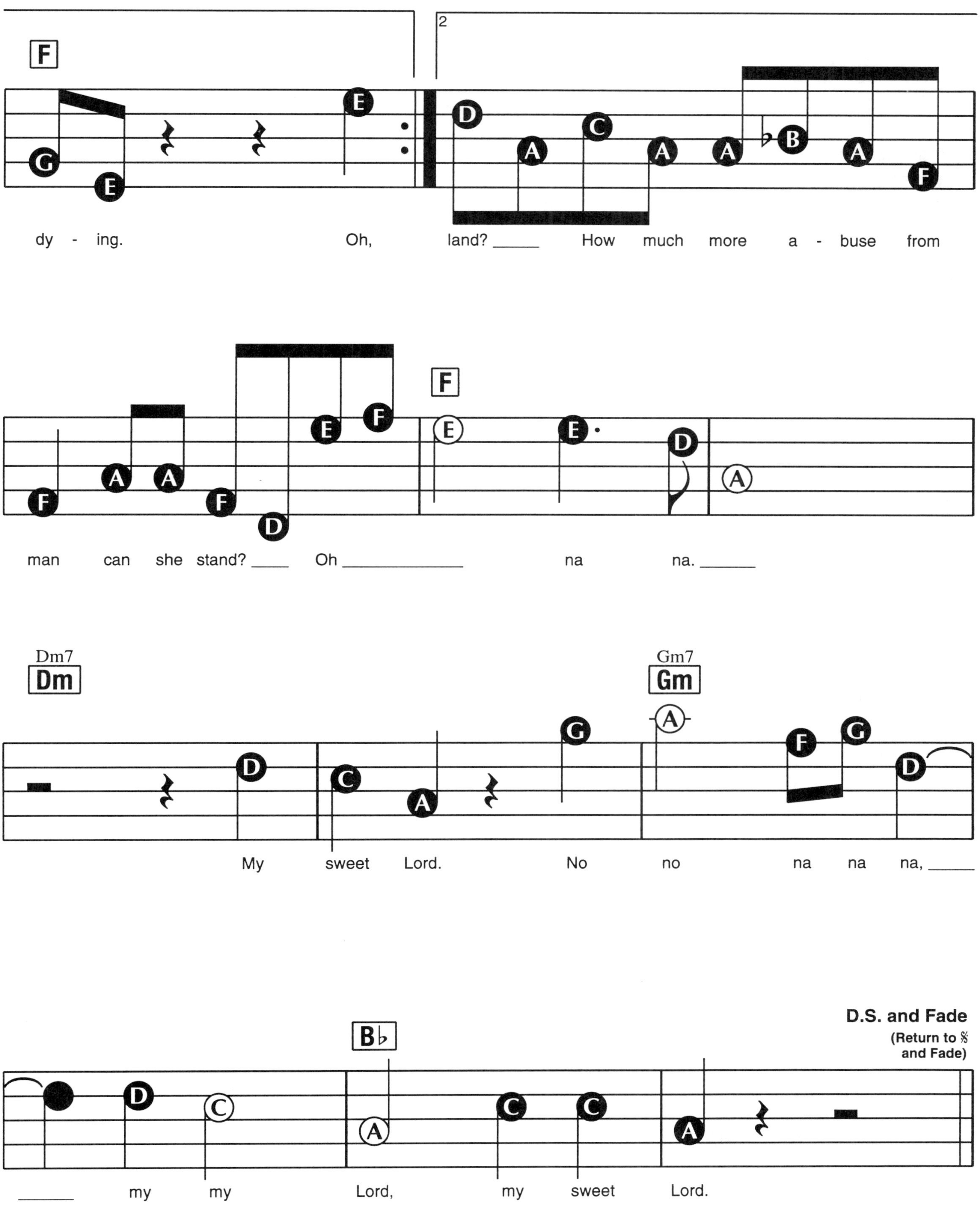
F
dy - ing. Oh,
2
land? How much more a - buse from
man can she stand? Oh
F
na na.
Dm7
Dm
My sweet Lord. No
Gm7
Gm
no na na na,
my my
B♭
Lord, my sweet Lord.
D.S. and Fade
(Return to 𝄋 and Fade)

My Girl

featured in the Motion Picture MY GIRL

Registration 9
Rhythm: Rock or 8 Beat

Words and Music by William "Smokey" Robinson
and Ronald White

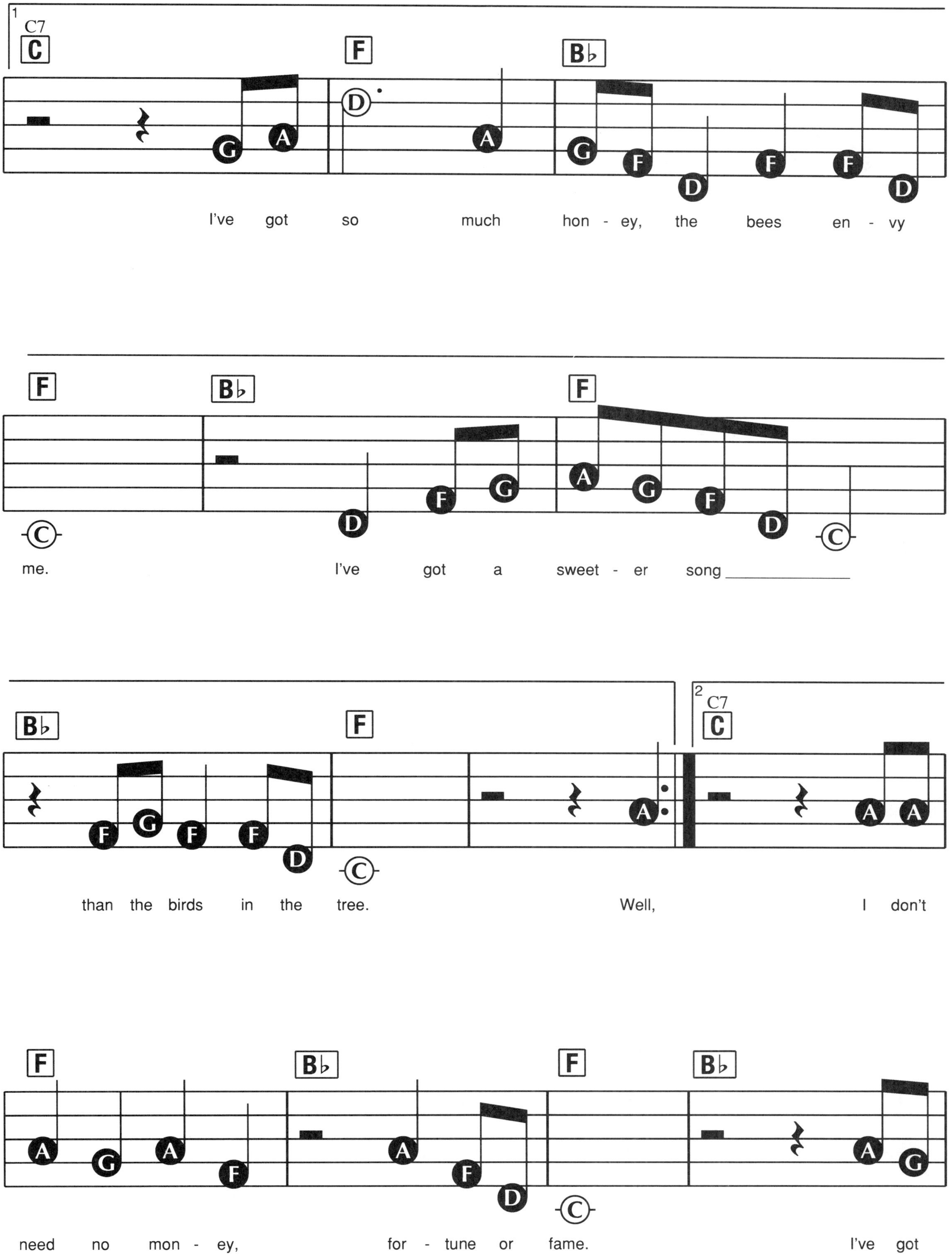
1
C7
C
F
B♭
I've got so much hon - ey, the bees en - vy
F
B♭
F
me.
I've got a sweet - er song
B♭
F
2
C7
C
than the birds in the tree.
Well, I don't
F
B♭
F
B♭
need no mon - ey, for - tune or fame.
I've got

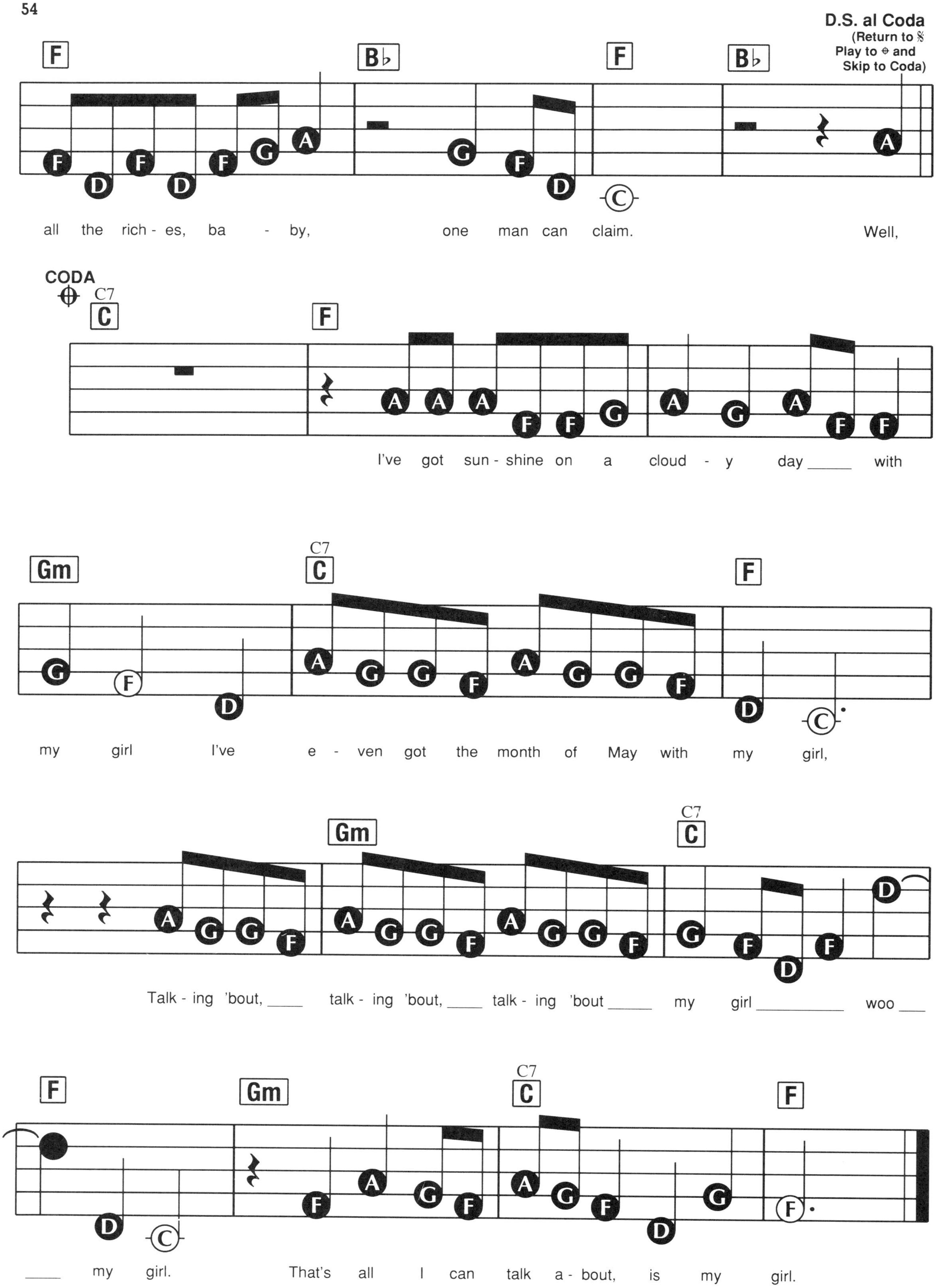
D.S. al Coda
(Return to 𝄋
Play to ⊕ and
Skip to Coda)
F
B♭
F
B♭
all the rich - es, ba - by, one man can claim. Well,
CODA
C7
C
F
I've got sun - shine on a cloud - y day ___ with
Gm
C7
C
F
my girl I've e - ven got the month of May with my girl,
Gm
C7
C
Talk - ing 'bout, ___ talk - ing 'bout, ___ talk - ing 'bout ___ my girl ___ woo ___
F
Gm
C7
C
F
___ my girl. That's all I can talk a - bout, is my girl.

Ooo Baby Baby

Registration 1
Rhythm: Rock or 8 Beat

Words and Music by William "Smokey" Robinson
and Warren Moore

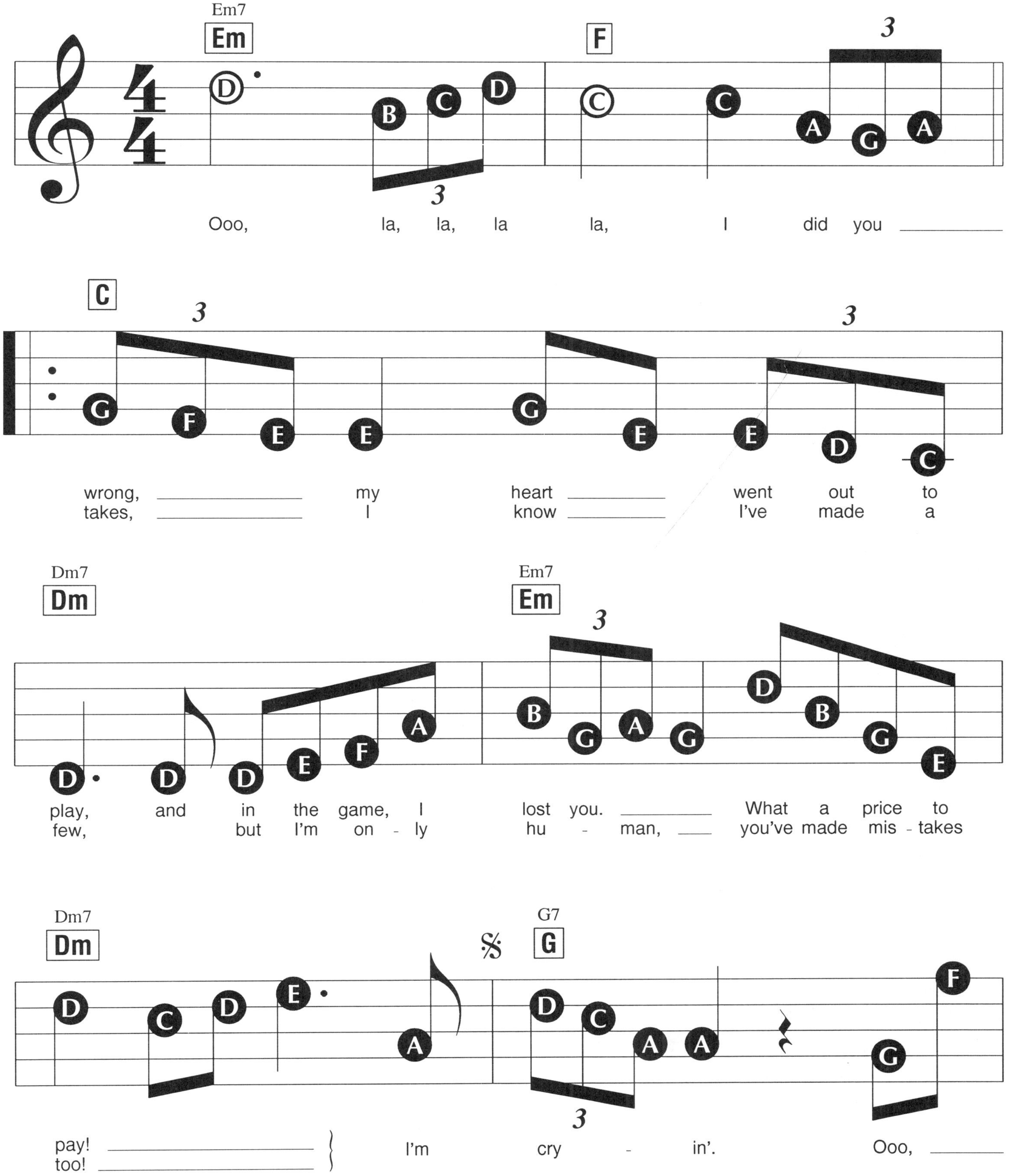

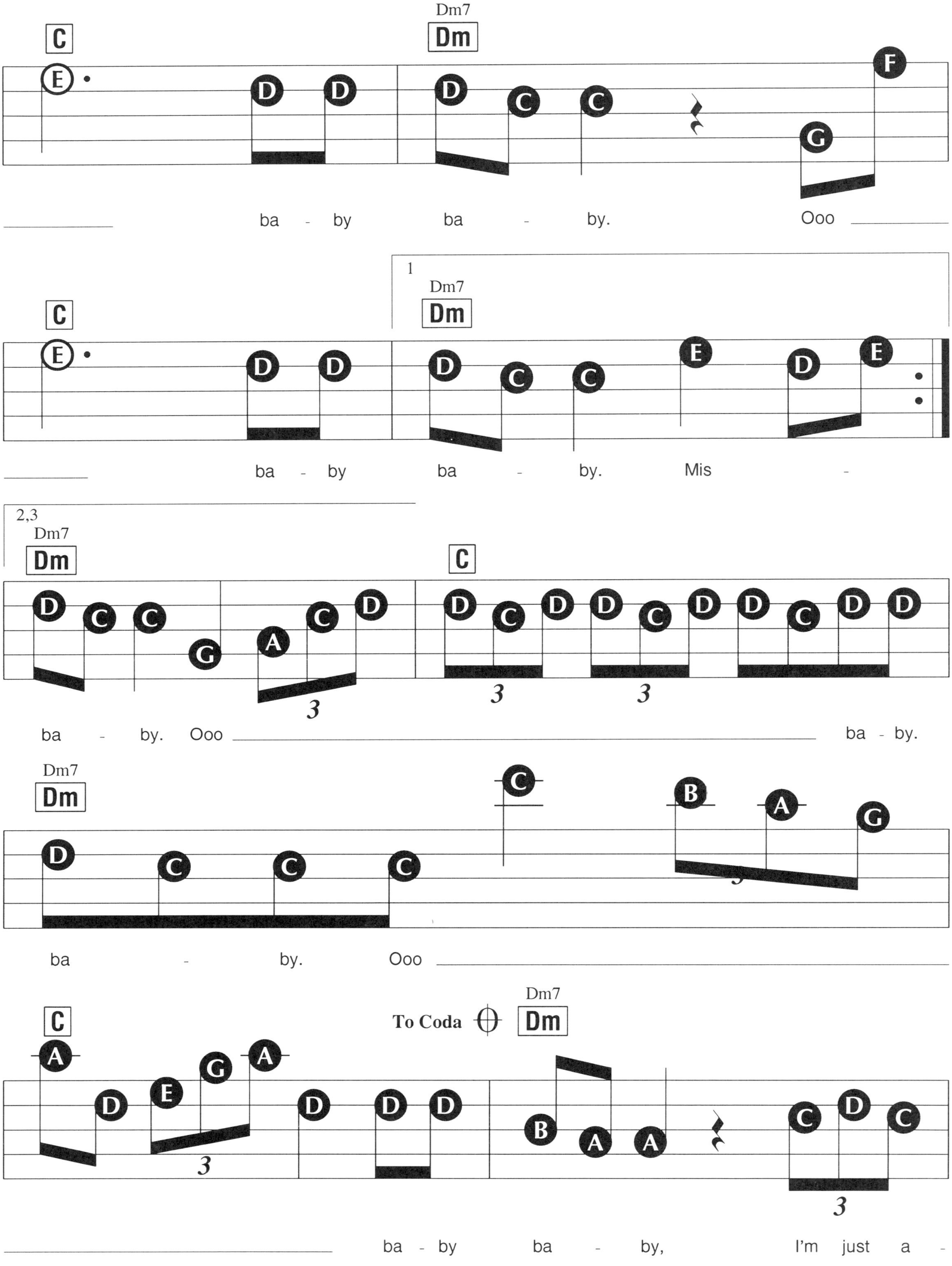
C Dm7 Dm
ba - by ba - by. Ooo
C 1 Dm7 Dm
ba - by ba - by. Mis -
2,3 Dm7 Dm C
ba - by. Ooo ba - by.
Dm7 Dm
ba - by. Ooo
C To Coda Dm7 Dm
ba - by ba - by, I'm just a -

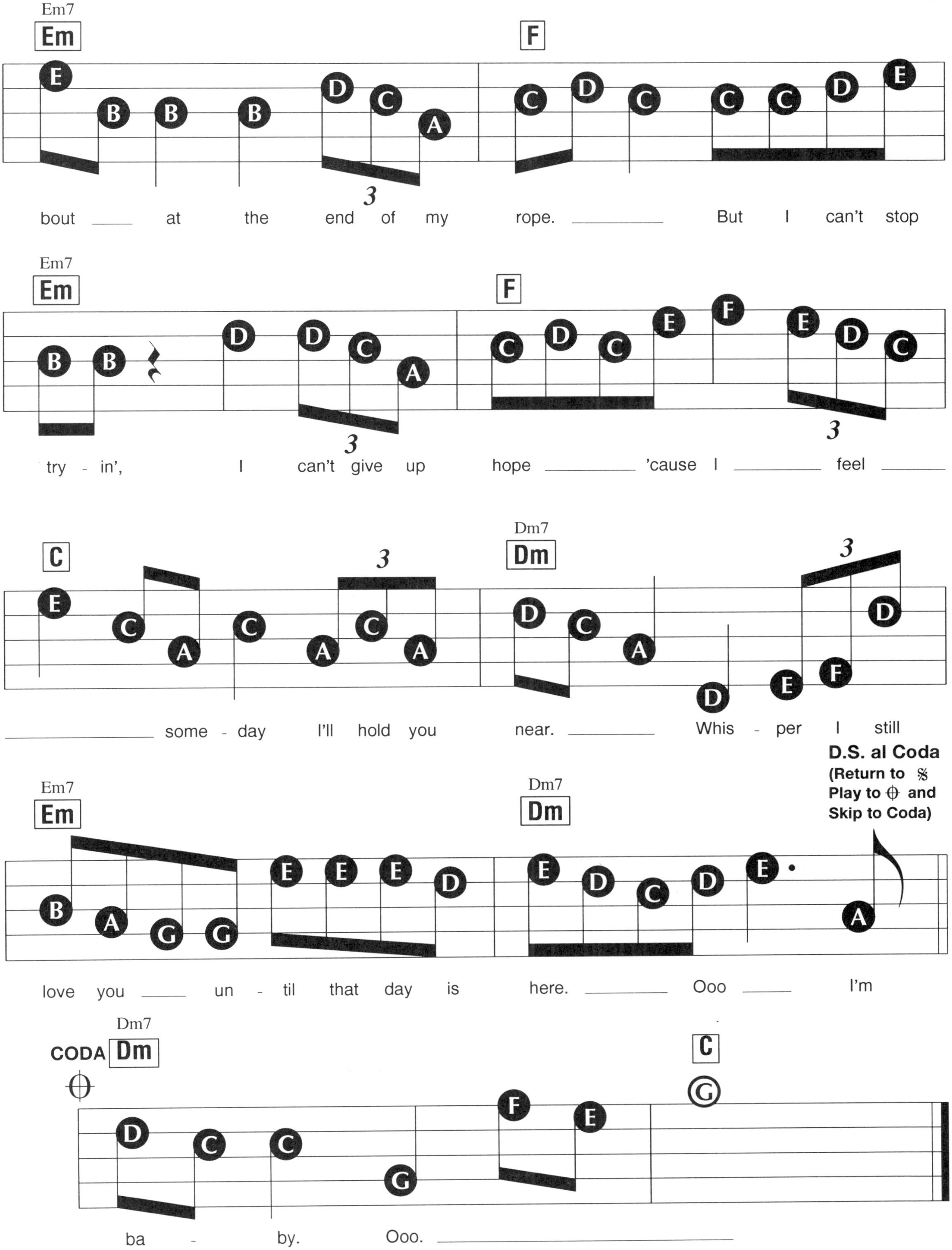
Em7 Em F
bout at the end of my rope. But I can't stop
Em7 Em F
try - in', I can't give up hope 'cause I feel
C Dm7 Dm
some - day I'll hold you near. Whis - per I still
Em7 Em Dm7 Dm
love you un - til that day is here. Ooo I'm
D.S. al Coda
(Return to 𝄋
Play to ⊕ and
Skip to Coda)
CODA Dm7 Dm C
ba - by. Ooo.

Never Can Say Goodbye

Registration 9
Rhythm: Disco or 16-Beat

Words and Music by
Clifton Davis

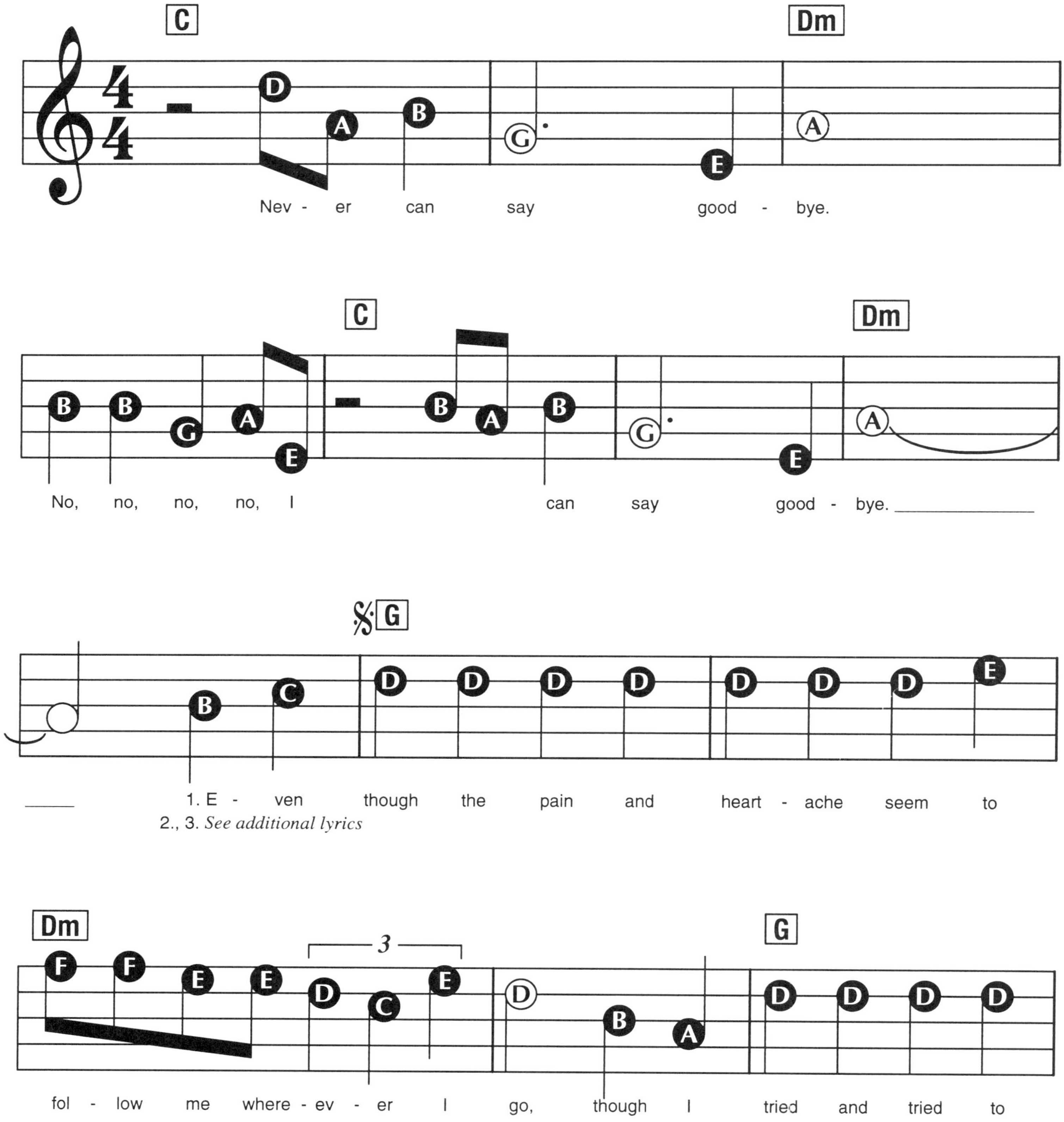

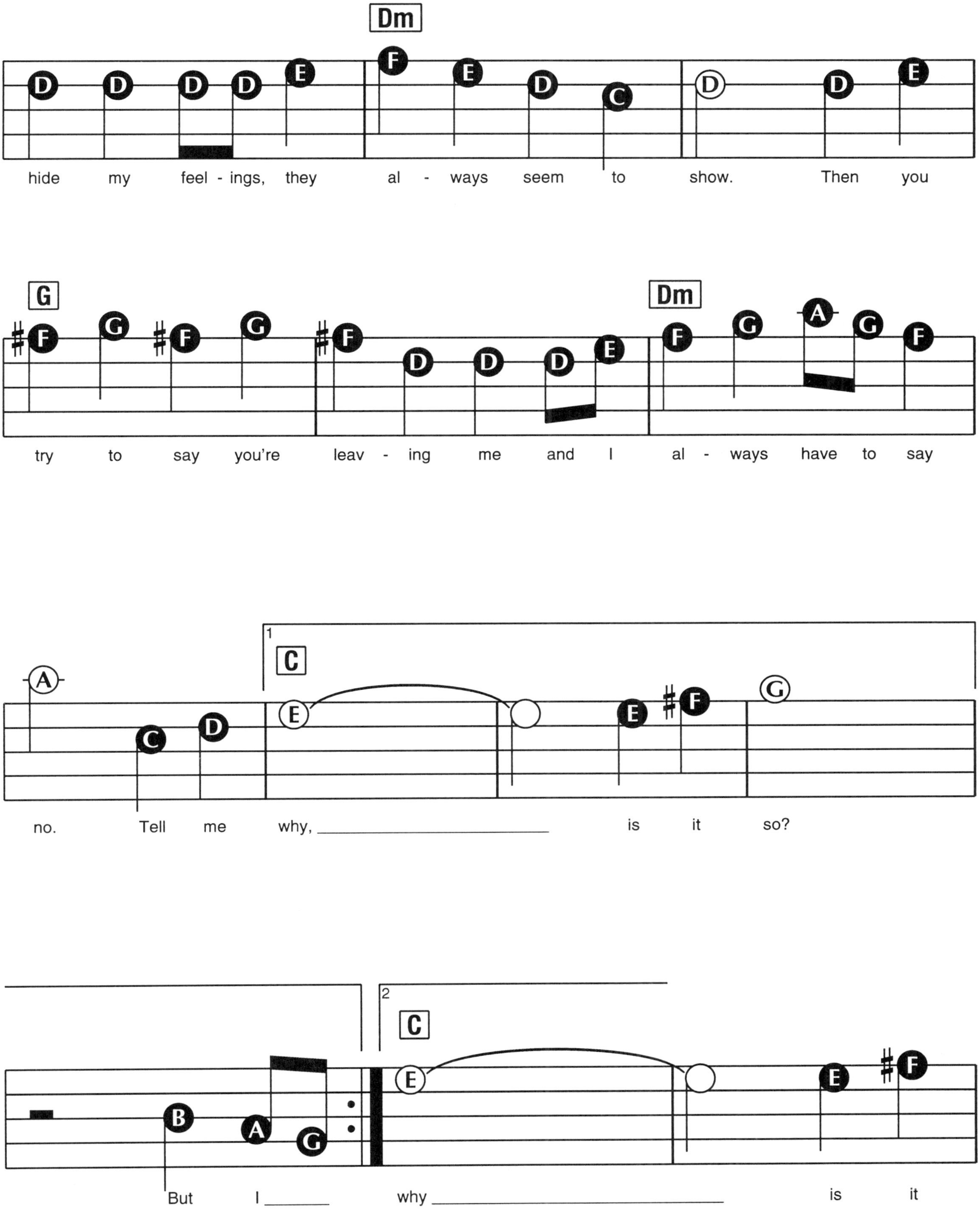
Dm
hide my feel - ings, they al - ways seem to show. Then you
G
Dm
try to say you're leav - ing me and I al - ways have to say
1
C
no. Tell me why, is it so?
2
C
But I why is it

G
so? Don't wan - na let you go. I
Gm
nev - er can say good - bye girl.
(boy.)
Don't wan - na let you
A7
A
G
go. I nev - er can say good - bye, no, no, no, no, no,
1
no. I nev - er can say good -

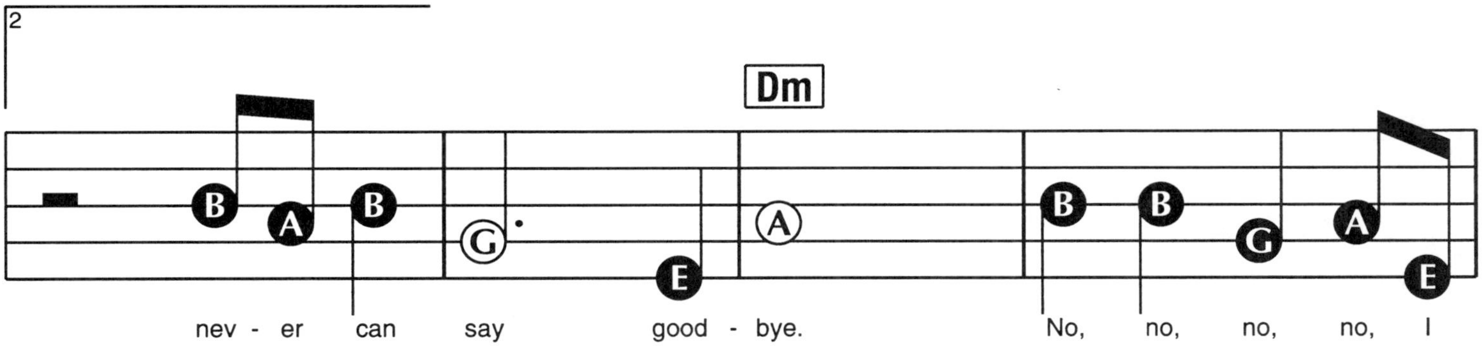

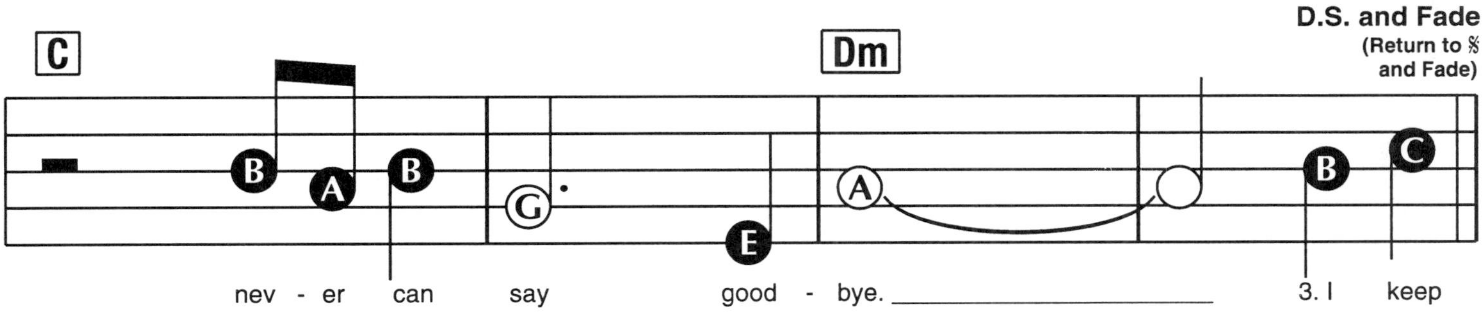

Additional Lyrics

2. Ev'ry time I think I've had enough and start heading for the door, there's very strange vibrations, piercing me right to the core. It says turn around, you fool, you know you love her more and more.

3. I keep thinkin' that our problems soon are all gonna work out, but there's that same unhappy feelin', there's that anguish, there's that doubt. It's that same old dizzy hang-up can't do with you or without.

Reach Out and Touch
(Somebody's Hand)

Registration 4
Rhythm: Waltz

Words and Music by Nickolas Ashford
and Valerie Simpson

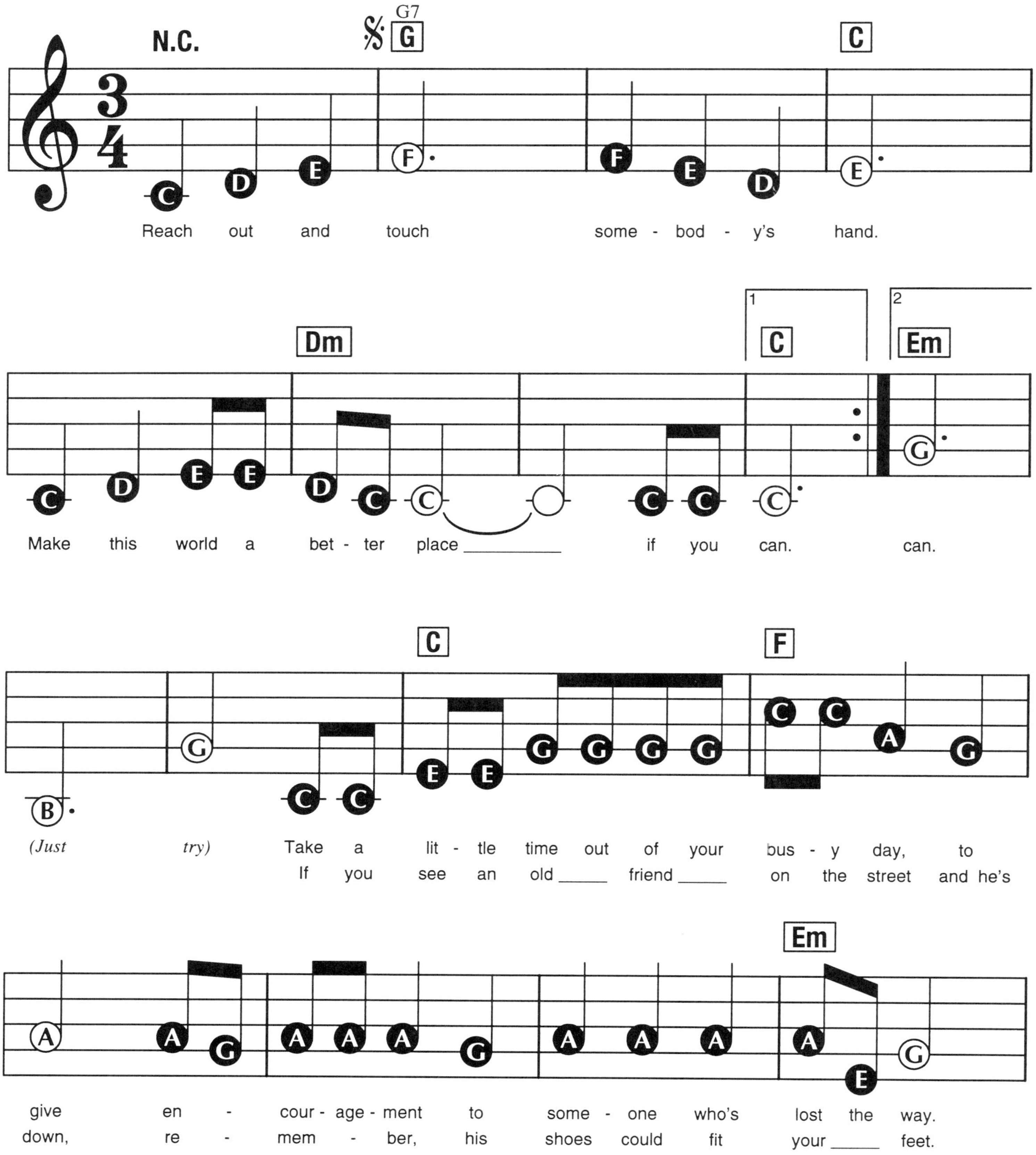

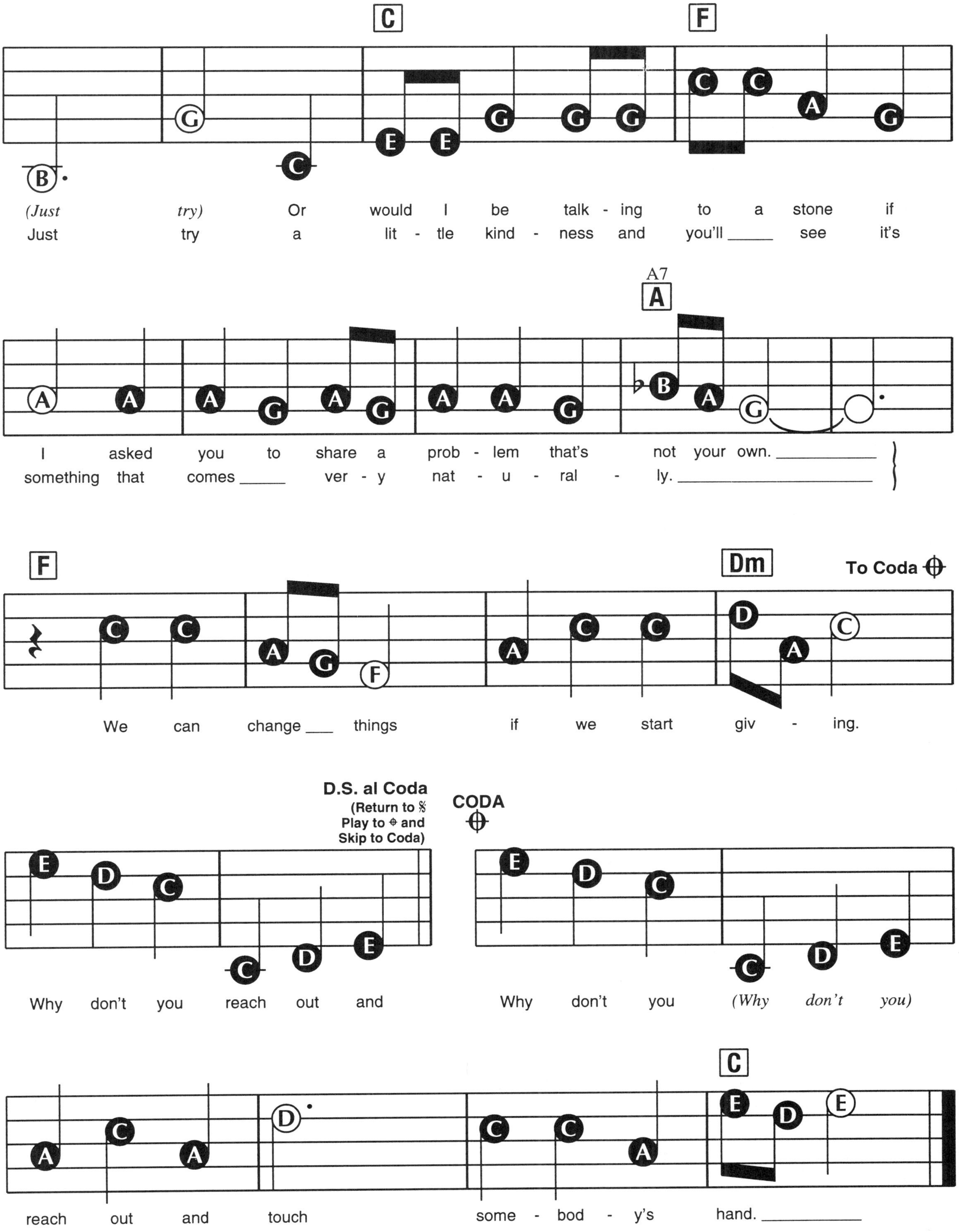
C
F
(Just try) Or would I be talk - ing to a stone if
Just try a lit - tle kind - ness and you'll ___ see it's
A7
A
I asked you to share a prob - lem that's not your own. ___
something that comes ___ ver - y nat - u - ral - ly. ___
F
Dm
To Coda
We can change ___ things if we start giv - ing.
D.S. al Coda
(Return to 𝄋 Play to ⊕ and Skip to Coda)
CODA
Why don't you reach out and
Why don't you (Why don't you)
C
reach out and touch some - bod - y's hand. ___

Smiling Faces Sometimes

Registration 4
Rhythm: Rock or 8 Beat

Words and Music by Norman Whitfield
and Barrett Strong

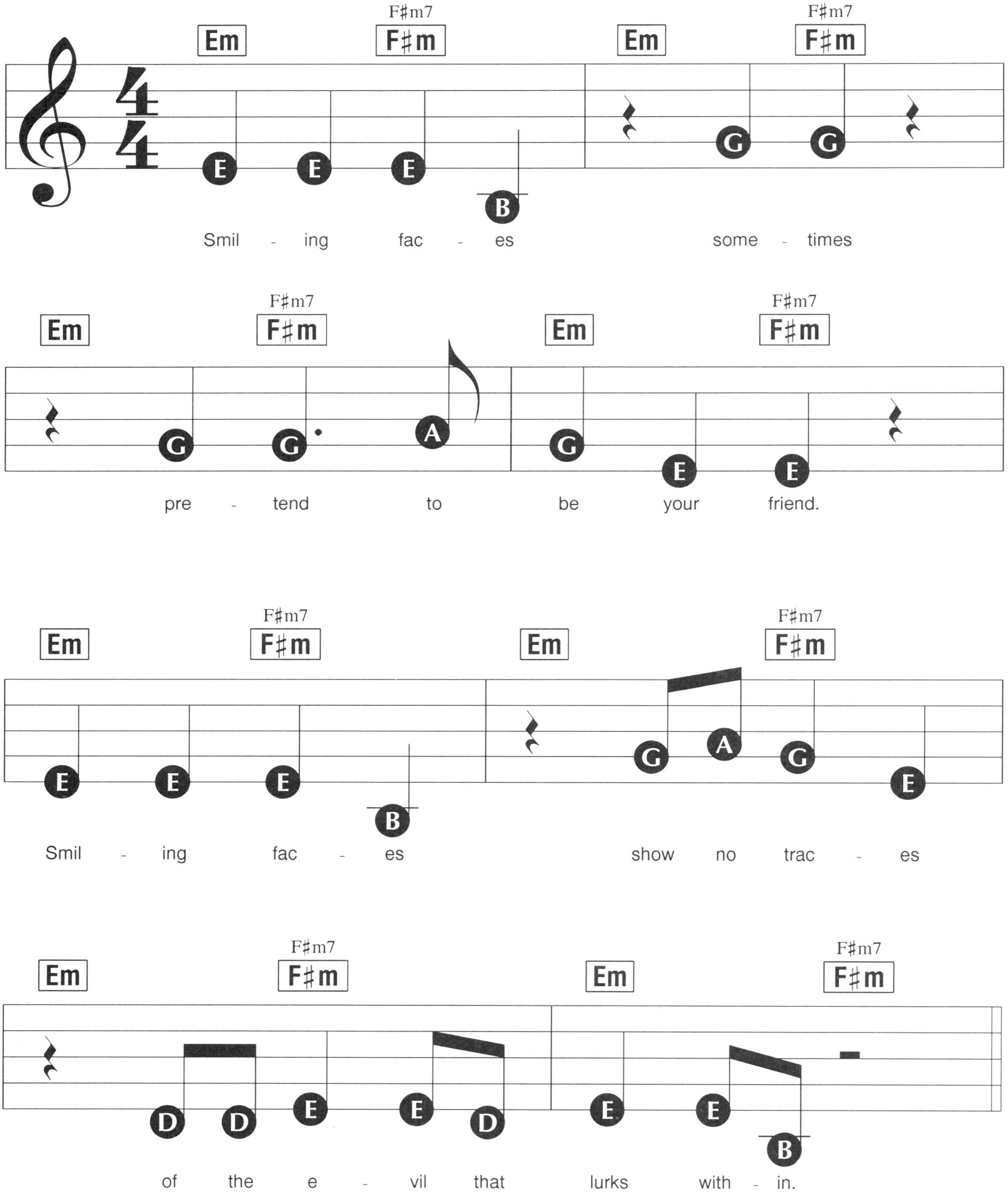

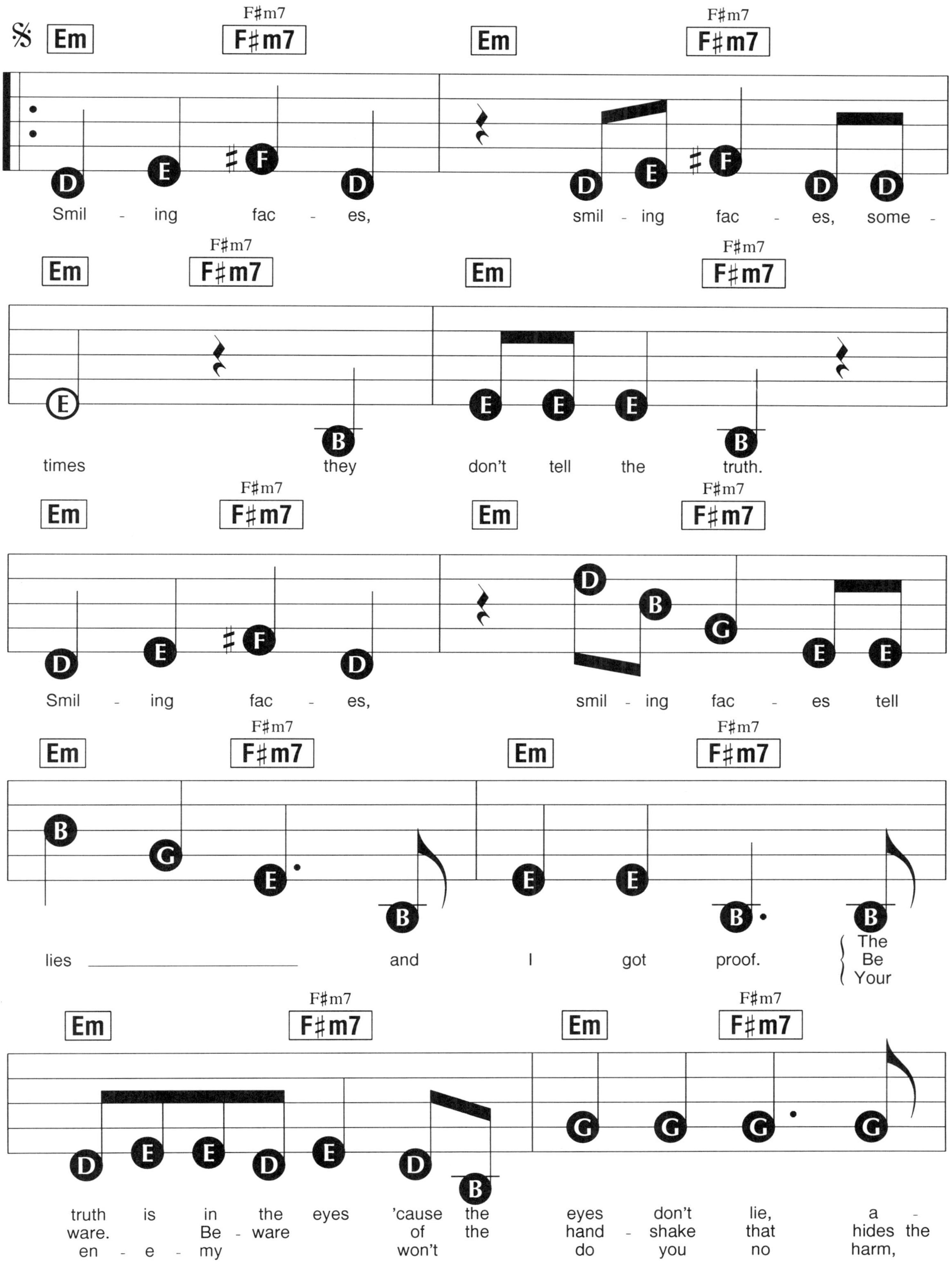
Em F♯m7 Em F♯m7
Smil - ing fac - es, smil - ing fac - es, some -
Em F♯m7 Em F♯m7
times they don't tell the truth.
Em F♯m7 Em F♯m7
Smil - ing fac - es, smil - ing fac - es tell
Em F♯m7 Em F♯m7
lies and I got proof.
The
Be
Your
Em F♯m7 Em F♯m7
truth is in the eyes 'cause the eyes don't lie, a -
ware. Be - ware of the hand - shake that hides the
en - e - my won't do you no harm,

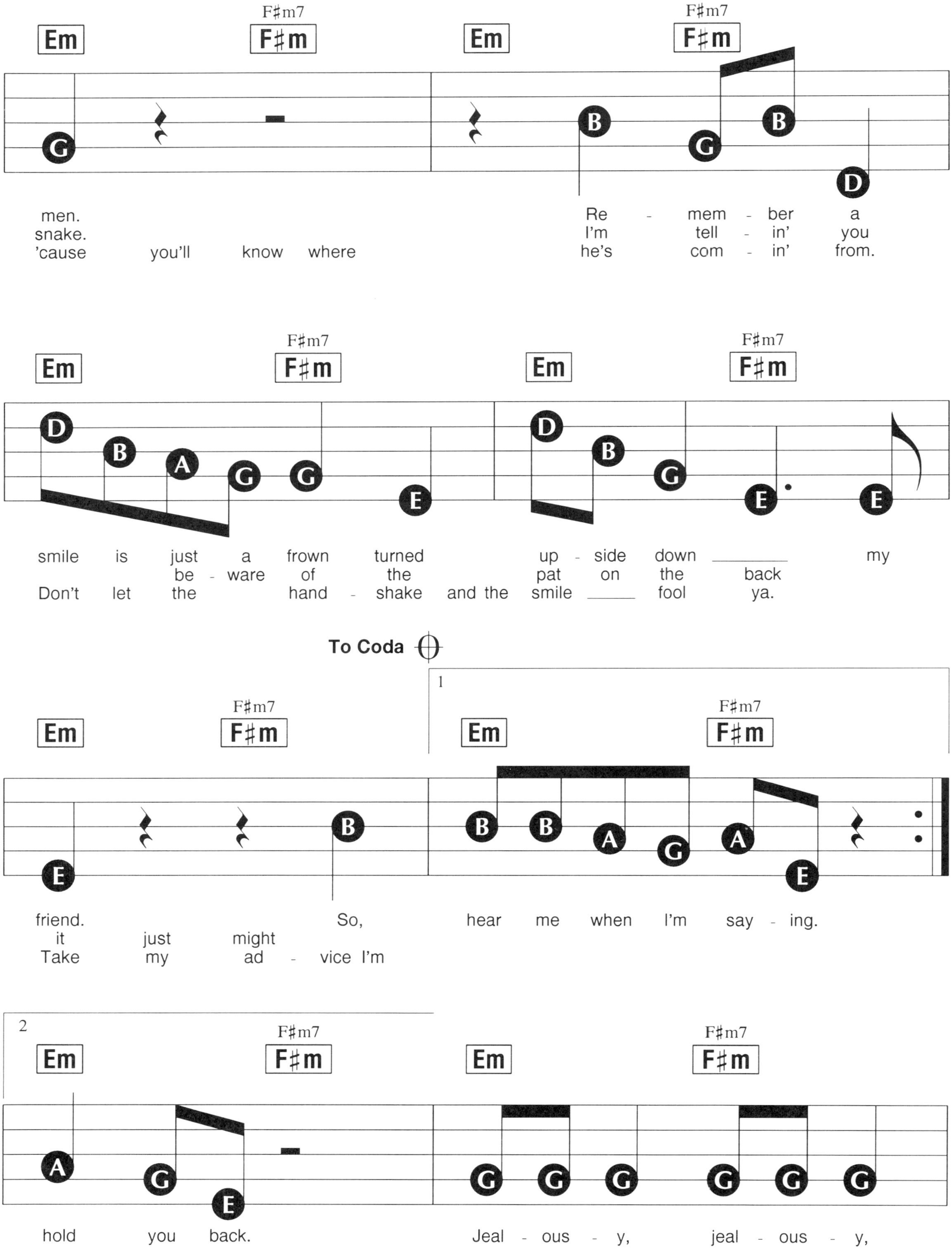
F♯m7 F♯m7
Em F♯m Em F♯m
men. Re - mem - ber a
snake. I'm tell - in' you
'cause you'll know where he's com - in' from.
F♯m7 F♯m7
Em F♯m Em F♯m
smile is just a frown turned up - side down my
be - ware of the pat on the back
Don't let the hand - shake and the smile fool ya.
To Coda
1
F♯m7 F♯m7
Em F♯m Em F♯m
friend. So, hear me when I'm say - ing.
it just might
Take my ad - vice I'm
2
F♯m7 F♯m7
Em F♯m Em F♯m
hold you back. Jeal - ous - y, jeal - ous - y,

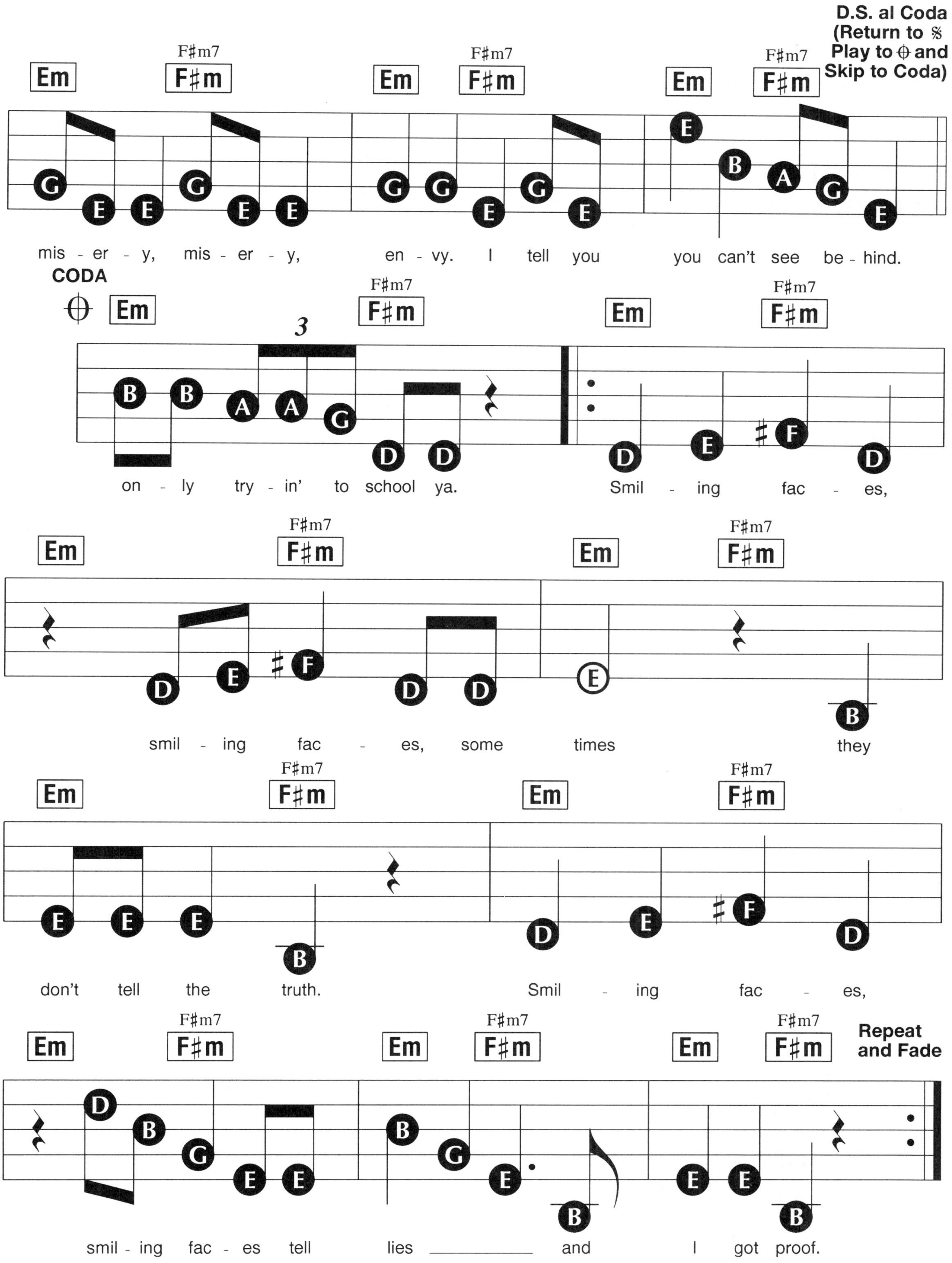
D.S. al Coda (Return to 𝄋 Play to ⊕ and Skip to Coda)
Em F#m7 F#m Em F#m7 F#m Em F#m7 F#m
mis - er - y, mis - er - y, en - vy. I tell you you can't see be - hind.
CODA
Em F#m7 F#m Em F#m7 F#m
on - ly try - in' to school ya. Smil - ing fac - es,
Em F#m7 F#m Em F#m7 F#m
smil - ing fac - es, some times they
Em F#m7 F#m Em F#m7 F#m
don't tell the truth. Smil - ing fac - es,
Em F#m7 F#m Em F#m7 F#m Em F#m7 F#m
Repeat and Fade
smil - ing fac - es tell lies and I got proof.

Someday We'll Be Together

Registration 2
Rhythm: Rock or 8 - Beat

Words and Music by Jackey Beavers,
Johnny Bristol and Harvey Fuqua

F
To Coda
C
B♭7
B♭
say some day we'll be to - geth -
F
C
er. Say some day we'll be to -
B♭7
B♭
F
B♭
geth - er. Long time a -
go, my my sweet thing, I made a
F
big mis - take, hon - ey. I

say, I said good - bye. Oh,
F7
F
B♭
oh, ba - by, ev - er ev - er
B♭m
3
ev - er since that day now now
G7
G
all I all I wan - na do ah is

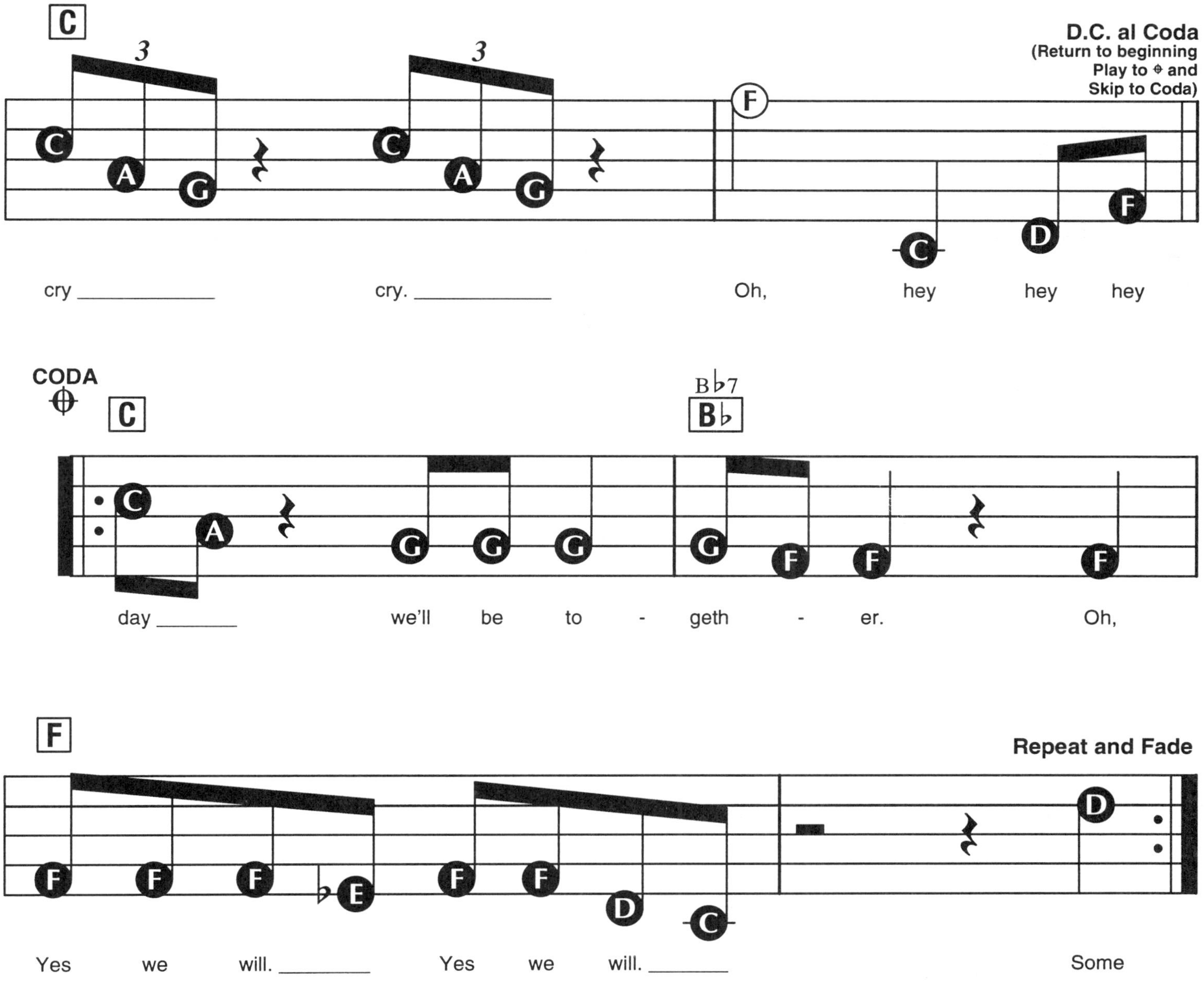

Additional Lyrics

2. You know my love is yours, baby,
 oh, right from the start
 You, you, you posess my soul now, honey.
 And I know, I know you own my heart.
 And I wanna say someday we'll be together.
 Yes we will, yes we will.
 I long for you, every night,
 just to kiss your sweet, sweet lips,
 Hold you ever so tight and I wanna say
 Someday we'll be together.
 Oh, yes we will, yes we will.

Still

Registration 9
Rhythm: Rock or 8 Beat

Words and Music by
Lionel Richie

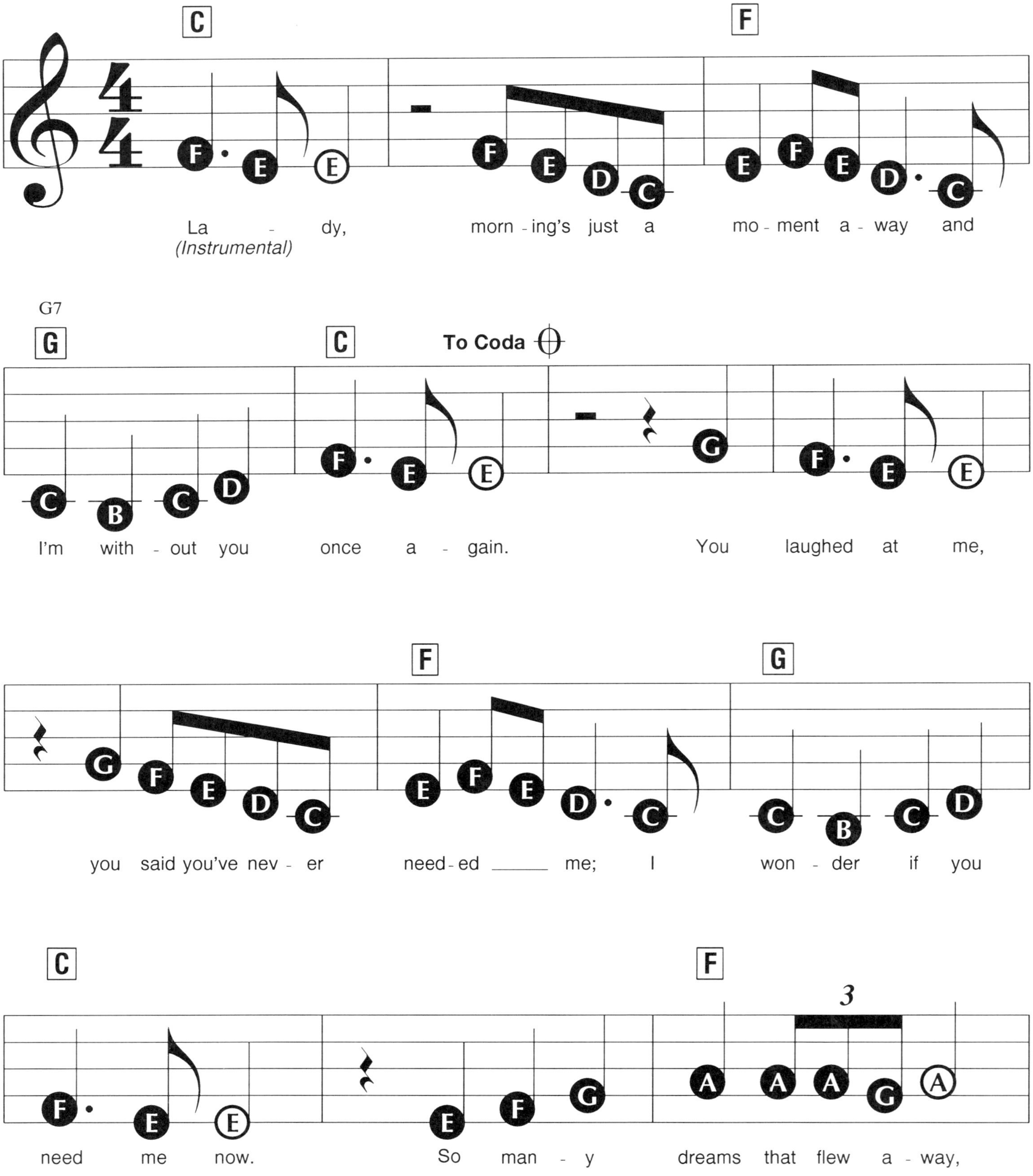

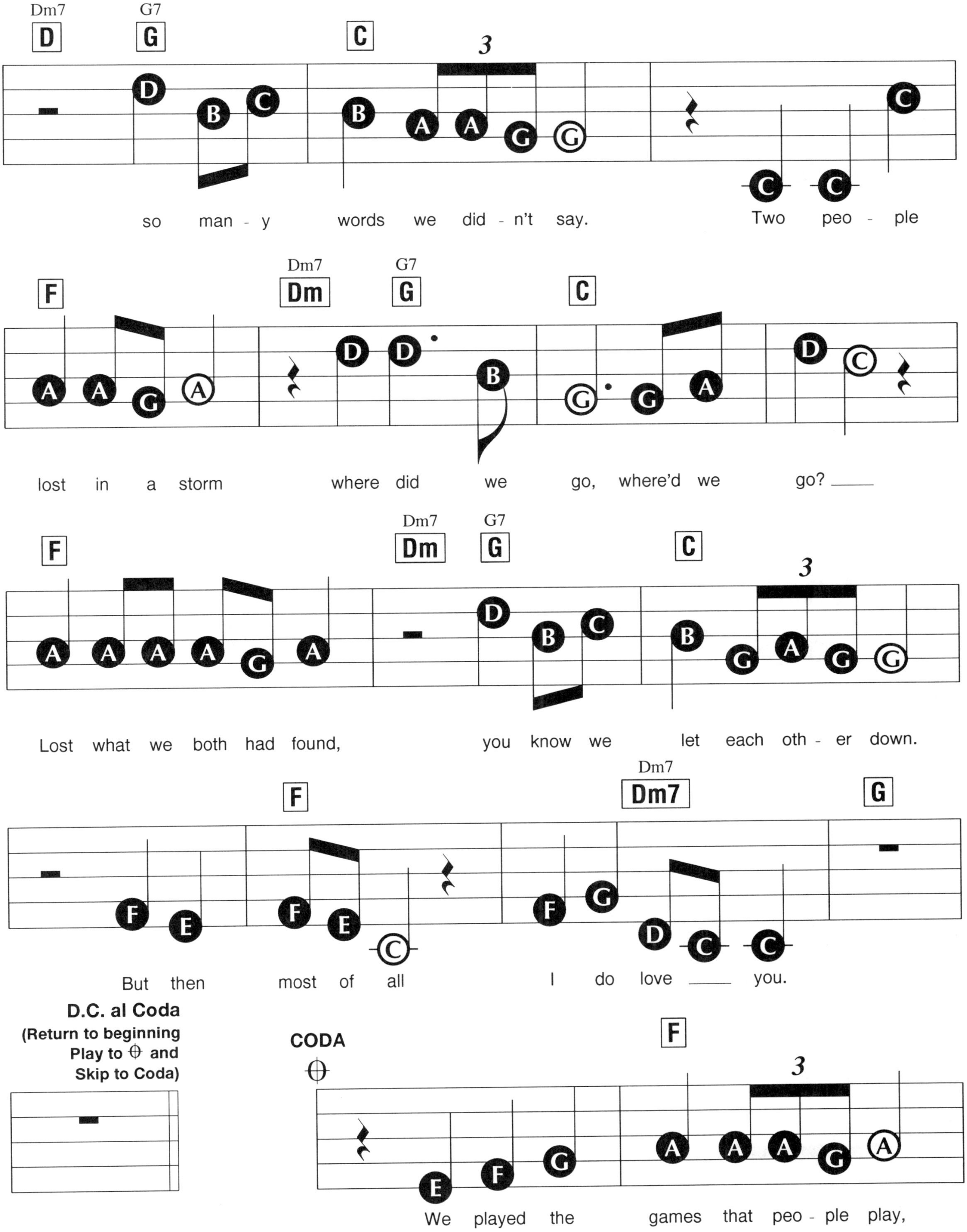
Dm7 G7
D G C
3
so man - y words we did - n't say. Two peo - ple
Dm7 G7
F Dm G C
lost in a storm where did we go, where'd we go?
Dm7 G7
F Dm G C
3
Lost what we both had found, you know we let each oth - er down.
Dm7
F Dm7 G
But then most of all I do love you.
D.C. al Coda
(Return to beginning
Play to ⊕ and
Skip to Coda)
CODA
⊕
F
3
We played the games that peo - ple play,

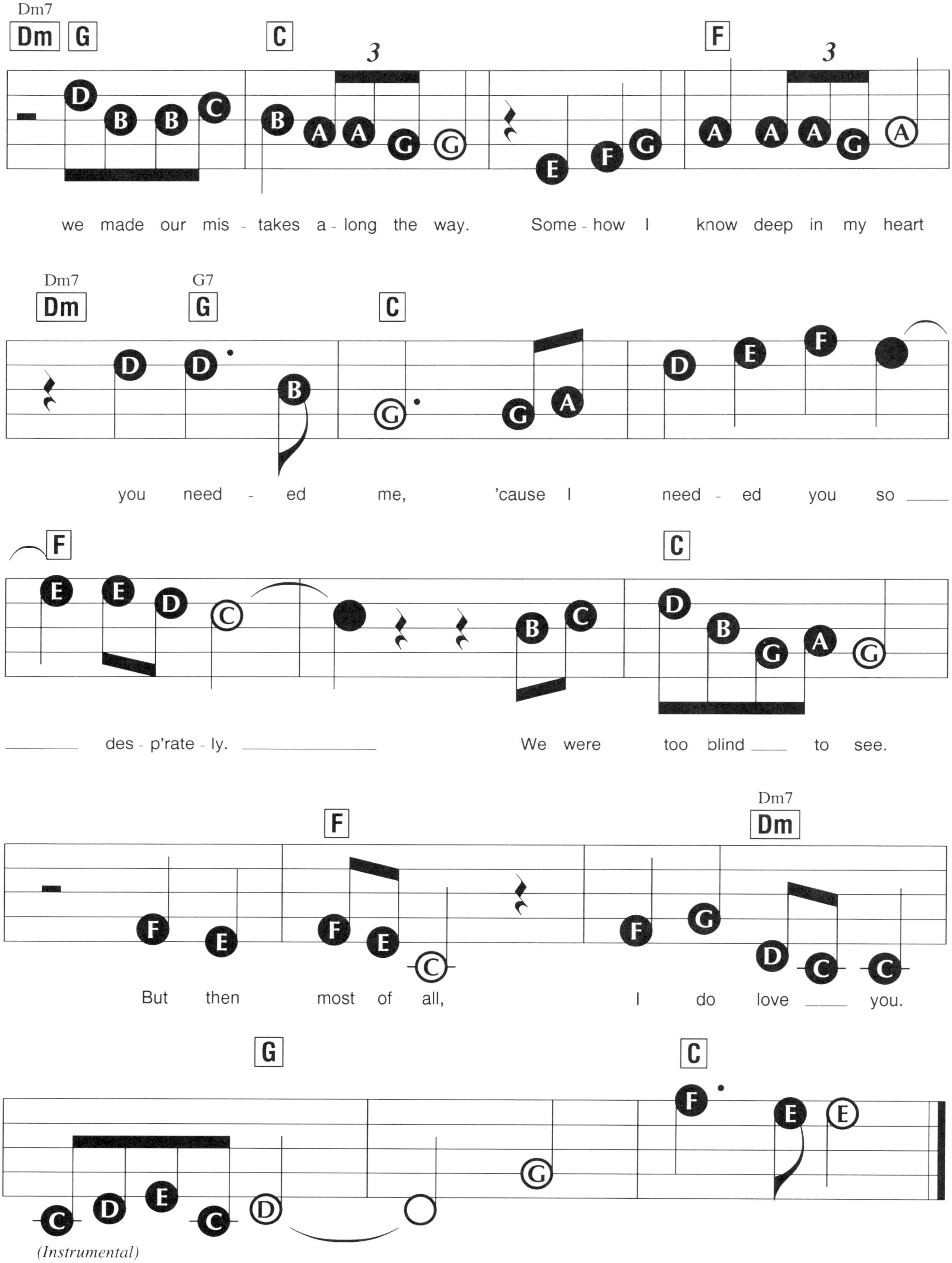
Dm7 Dm G
C
F
we made our mis - takes a - long the way.
Some - how I know deep in my heart
Dm7 Dm
G7 G
C
you need - ed me, 'cause I need - ed you so
F
C
des - p'rate - ly.
We were too blind to see.
F
Dm7 Dm
But then most of all,
I do love you.
G
C
(Instrumental)

Three Times a Lady

Registration 1
Rhythm: Waltz

Words and Music by
Lionel Richie

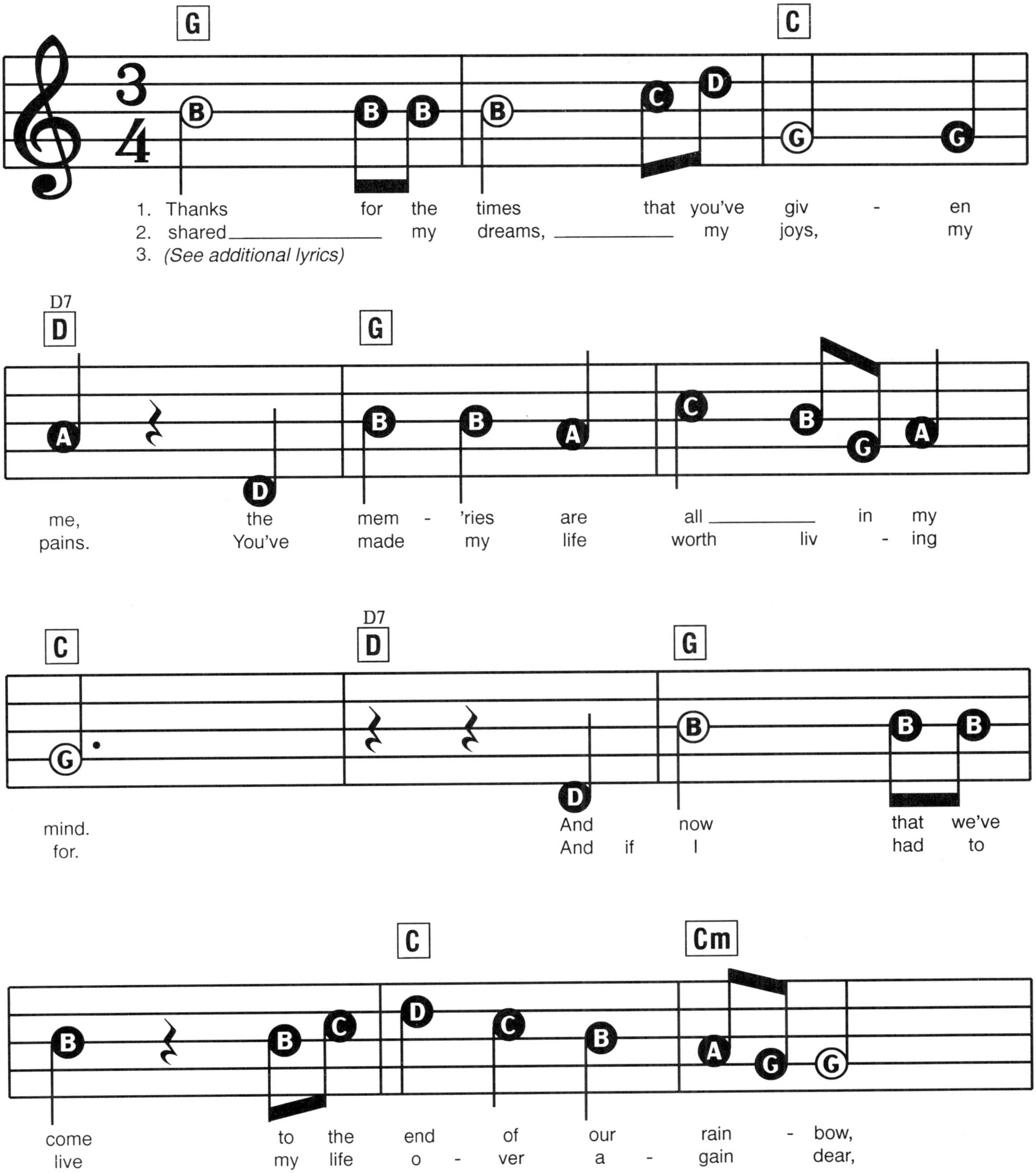

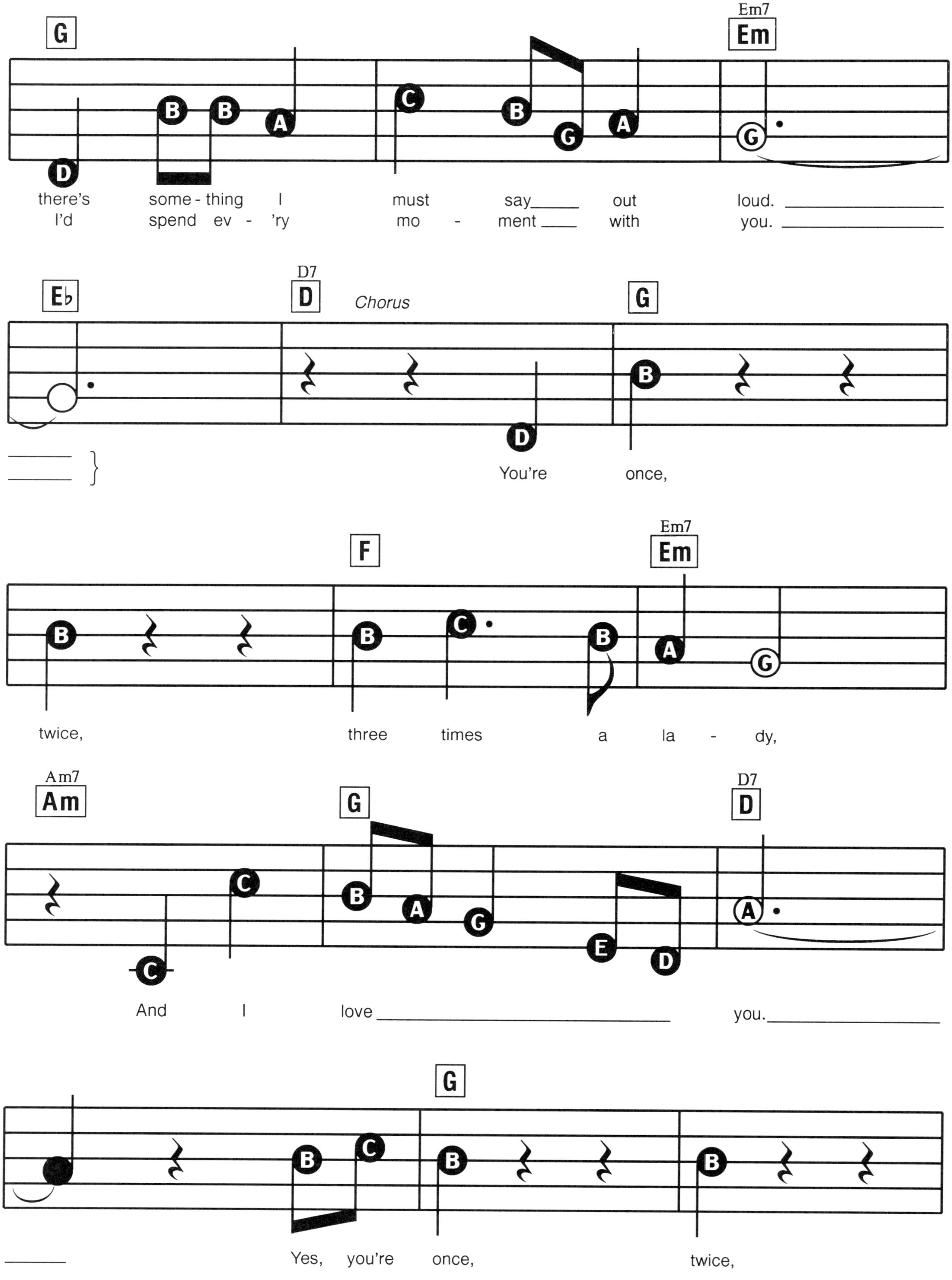
G
Em7
Em
there's some - thing I must say out loud.
I'd spend ev - 'ry mo - ment with you.
E♭
D7
D
Chorus
G
You're once,
F
Em7
Em
twice, three times a la - dy,
Am7
Am
G
D7
D
And I love you.
G
Yes, you're once, twice,

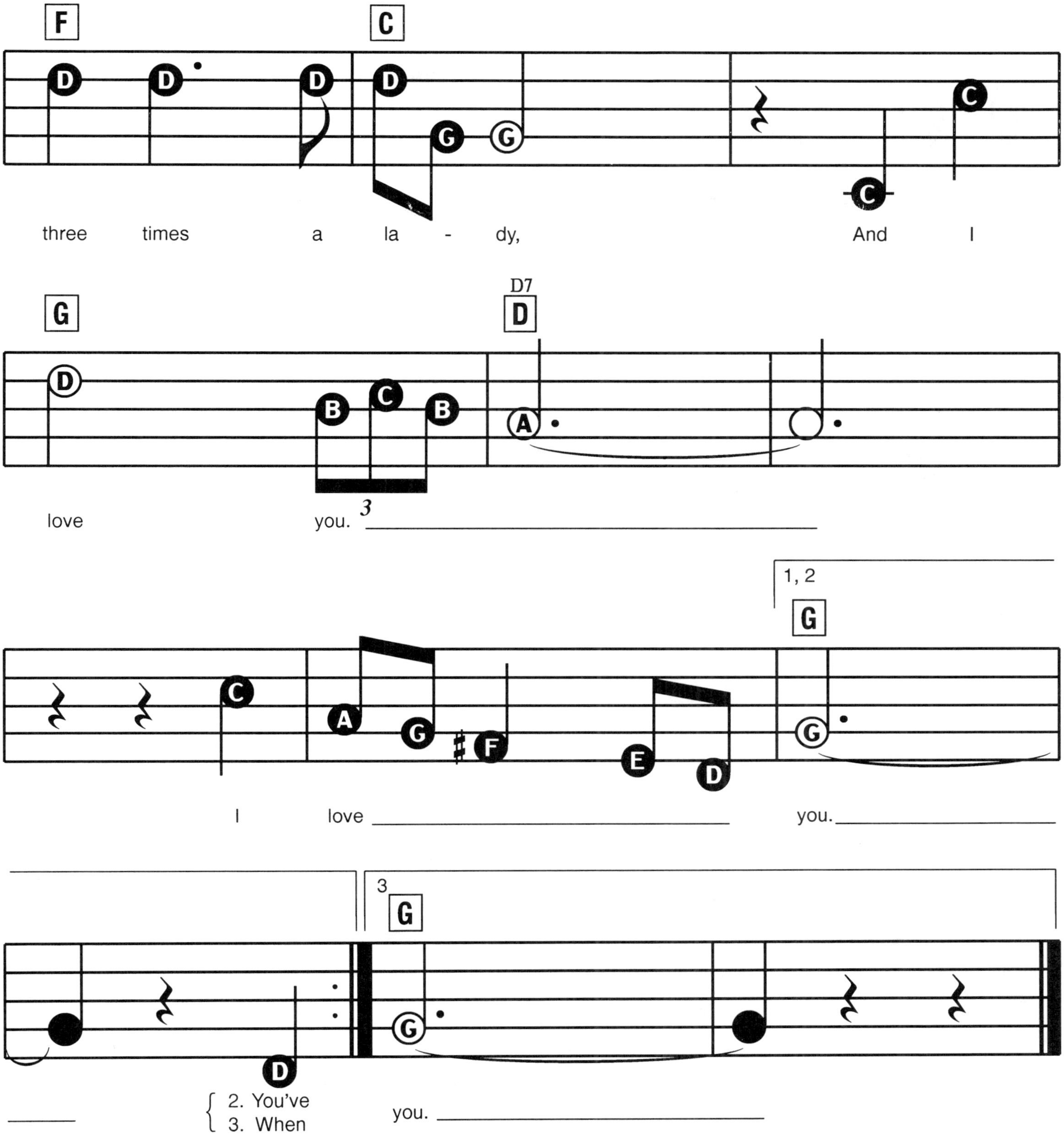

Additional Lyrics

3. When we are together the moments I cherish
With ev'ry beat of my heart.
To touch you, to hold you, to feel you, to need you.
There's nothing to keep us apart.
Chorus

Time Will Reveal

Registration 7
Rhythm: Rock or 8 Beat

Words and Music by Bunny DeBarge
and Eldra DeBarge

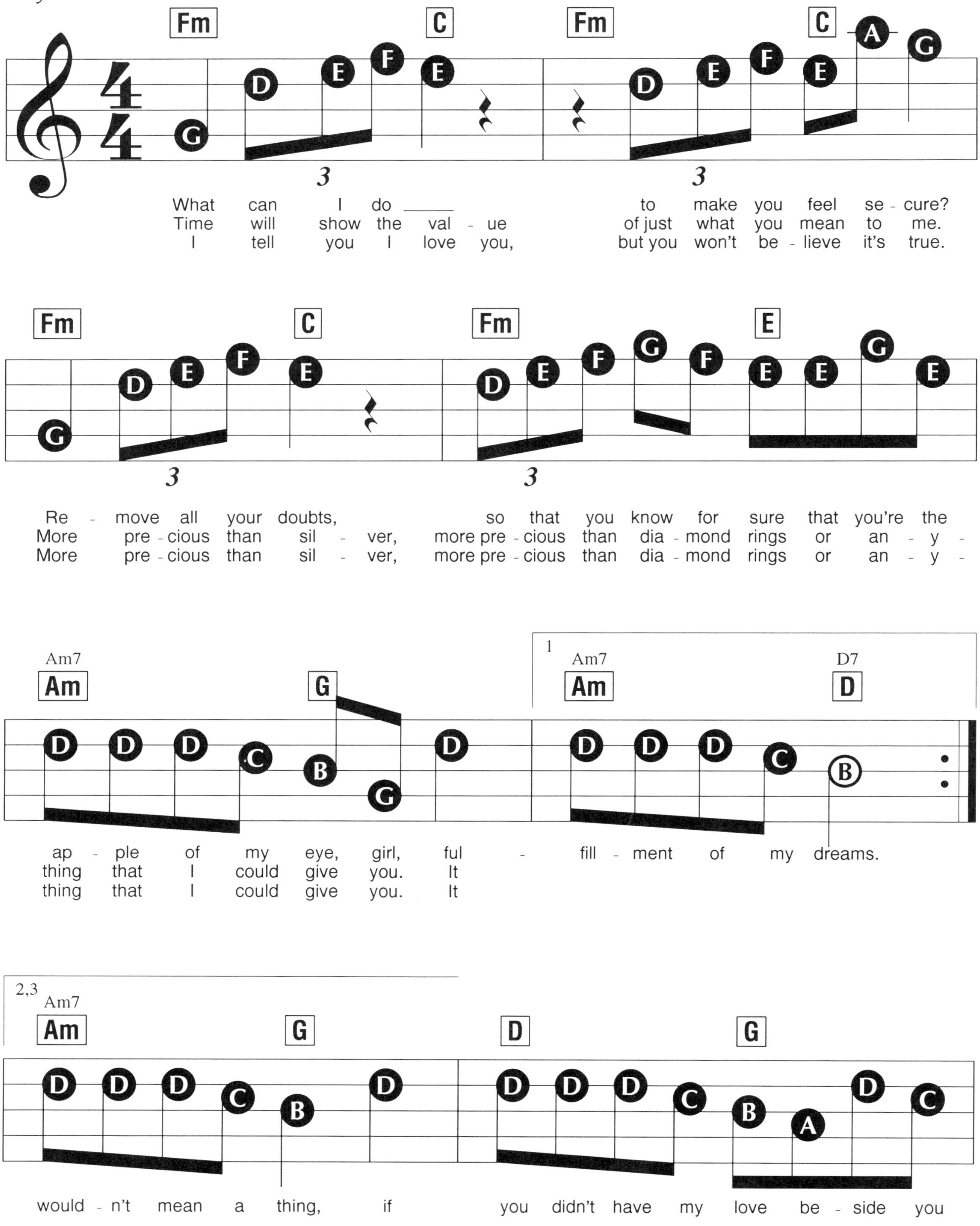

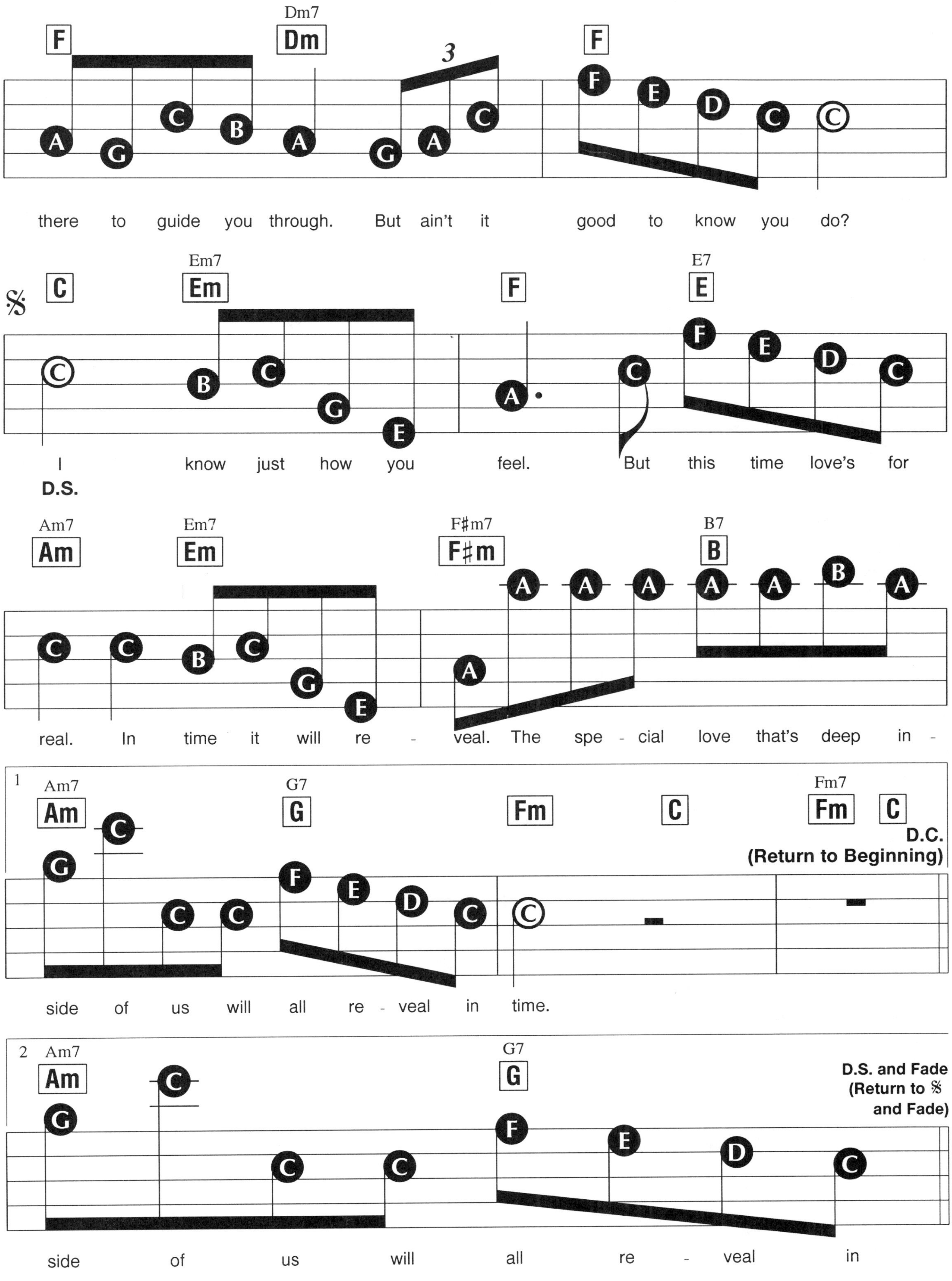
F Dm7 Dm F
A G C B A G A C F E D C C
3
there to guide you through. But ain't it good to know you do?
C Em7 Em F E7 E
C B C G E A C F E D C
I know just how you feel. But this time love's for
D.S.
Am7 Am Em7 Em F♯m7 F♯m B7 B
C C B C G E A A A A A A B A
real. In time it will re - veal. The spe - cial love that's deep in -
1 Am7 Am G7 G Fm C Fm7 Fm C
G C C C F E D C C
D.C.
(Return to Beginning)
side of us will all re - veal in time.
2 Am7 Am G7 G
G C C C F E D C
D.S. and Fade
(Return to 𝄋
and Fade)
side of us will all re - veal in

Touch Me in the Morning

Registration 1
Rhythm: Rock or 8 Beat

Words and Music by Ronald Miller
and Michael Masser

C
F
(Hey!) Was - n't it me who said that noth - in' good's gon - na last for -
(Hey!) Was - n't it yes - ter - day we used to laugh at the wind be -
C
ev - er? And was - n't it me who said let's just be
hind us? Did - n't we run a - way and hope that
F
G
glad for the time to - geth - er? Must - 've been
time would - n't try to find us? Did - n't we
B♭
hard to tell me, that you've giv - en all you had to give.
take each oth - er, to a place where no one's ev - er been?
G
B♭
I can un - der - stand your feel - in' that way. Ev - 'ry - bod - y's
Yeah, I real - ly need you near me to - night. 'Cause you'll nev - er

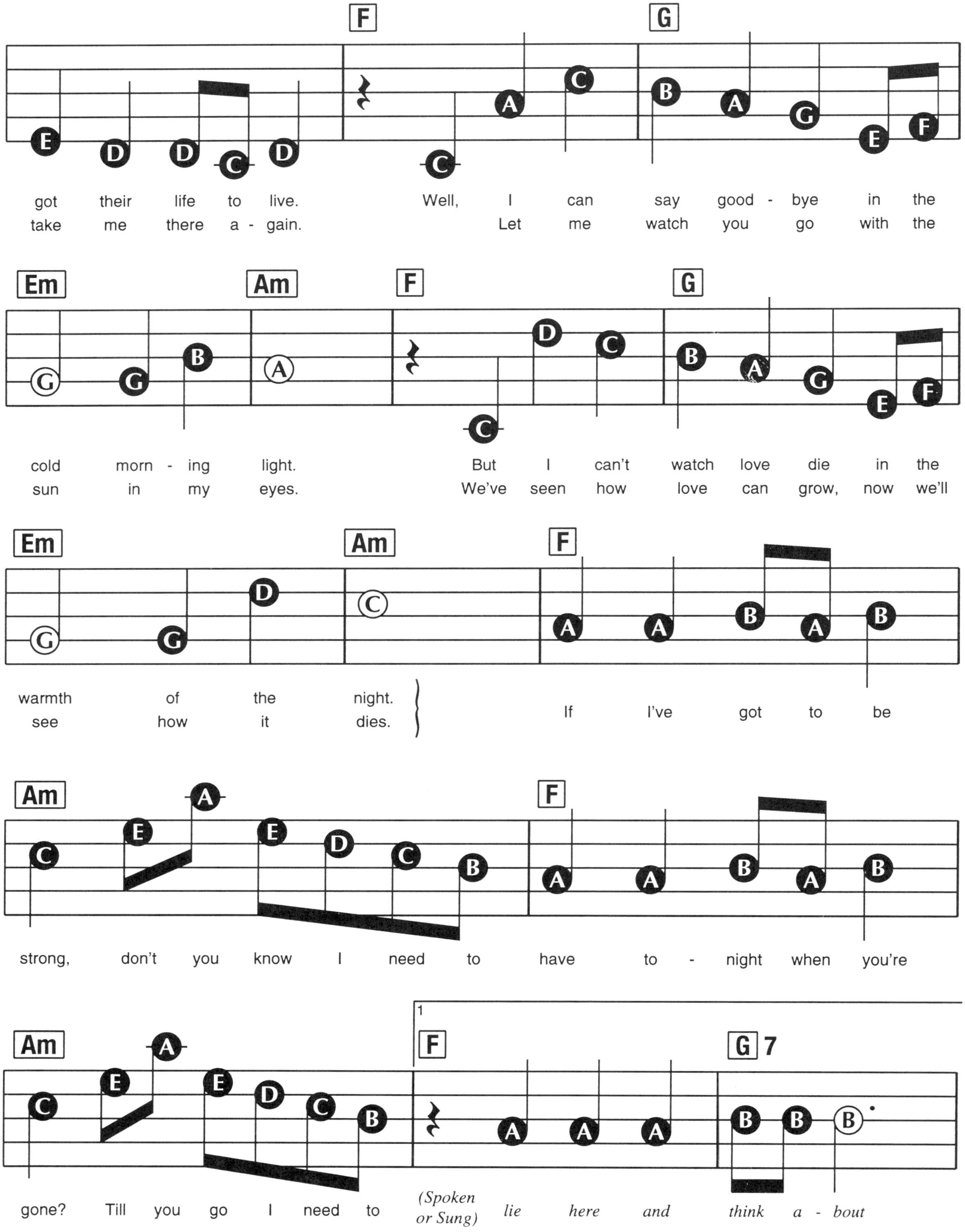
F G
got their life to live. Well, I can say good - bye in the
take me there a - gain. Let me watch you go with the
Em Am F G
cold morn - ing light. But I can't watch love die in the
sun in my eyes. We've seen how love can grow, now we'll
Em Am F
warmth of the night.
see how it dies.
If I've got to be
Am F
strong, don't you know I need to have to - night when you're
Am 1 F G7
gone? Till you go I need to
(Spoken or Sung) lie here and think a - bout

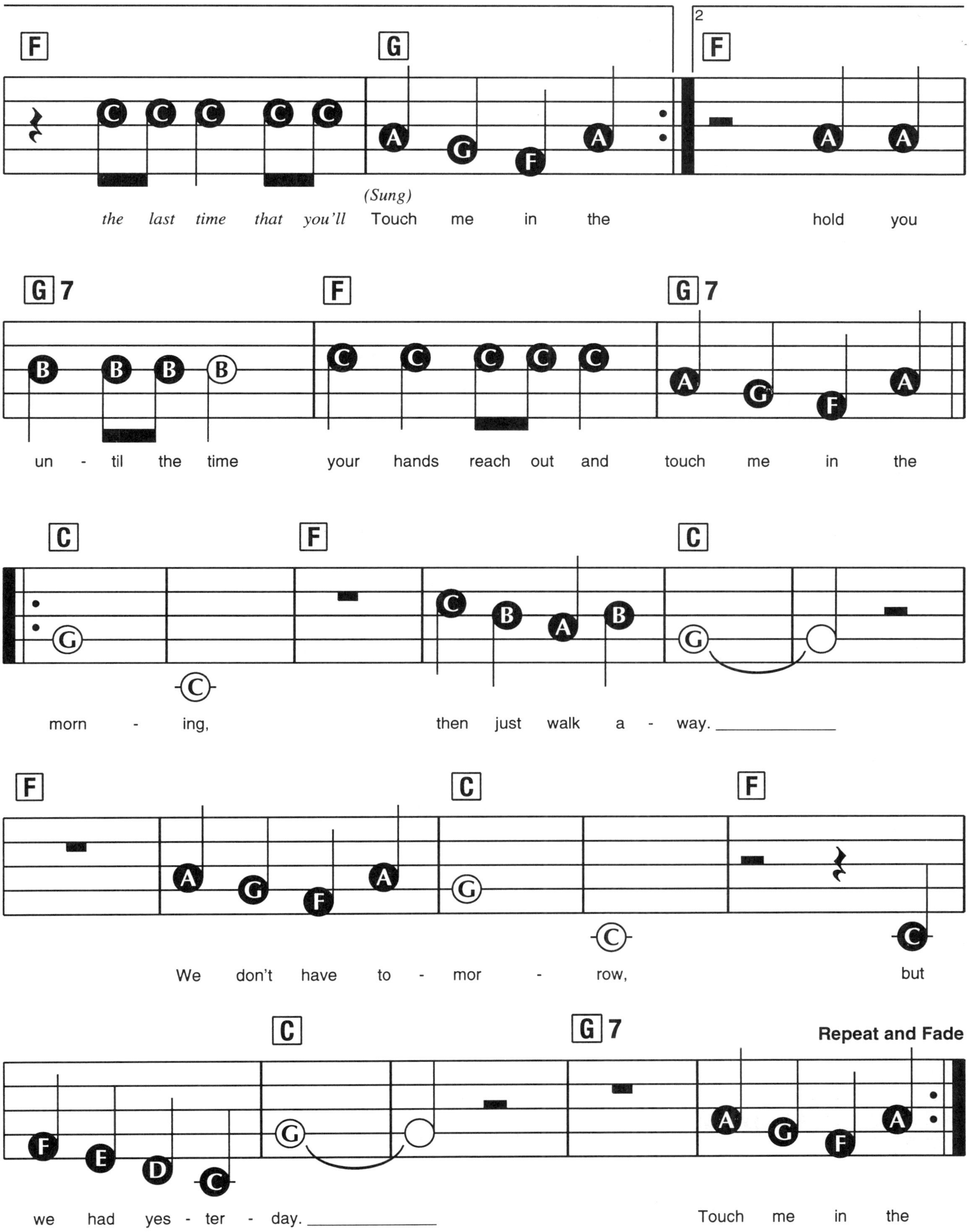
F
G
2
F
the last time that you'll
(Sung)
Touch me in the
hold you
G7
F
G7
un - til the time
your hands reach out and
touch me in the
C
F
C
morn - ing,
then just walk a - way.
F
C
F
We don't have to - mor - row,
but
C
G7
Repeat and Fade
we had yes - ter - day.
Touch me in the

The Tracks of My Tears

Registration 2
Rhythm: Rock or 8 Beat

Words and Music by William "Smokey" Robinson,
Warren Moore and Marvin Tarplin

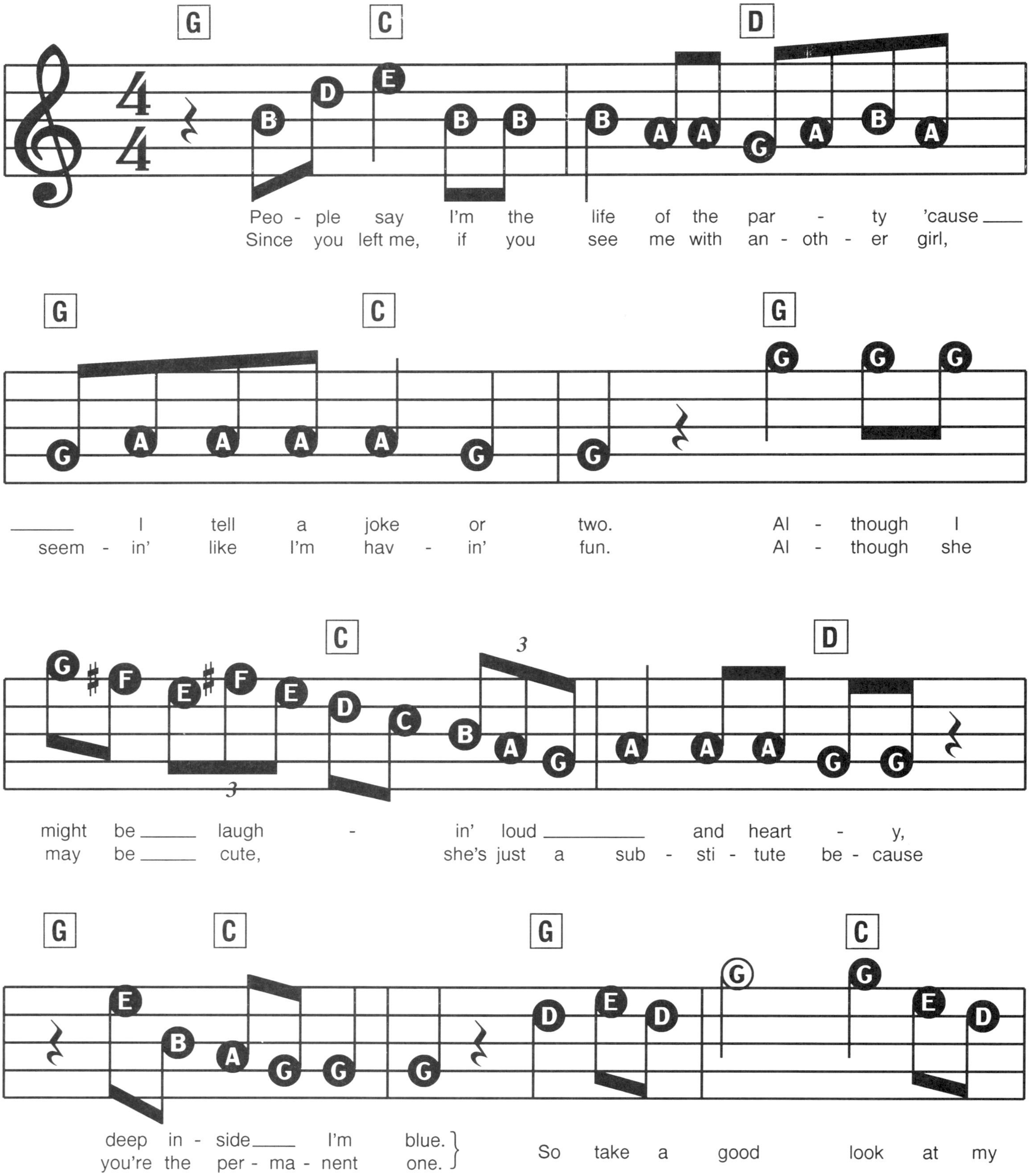

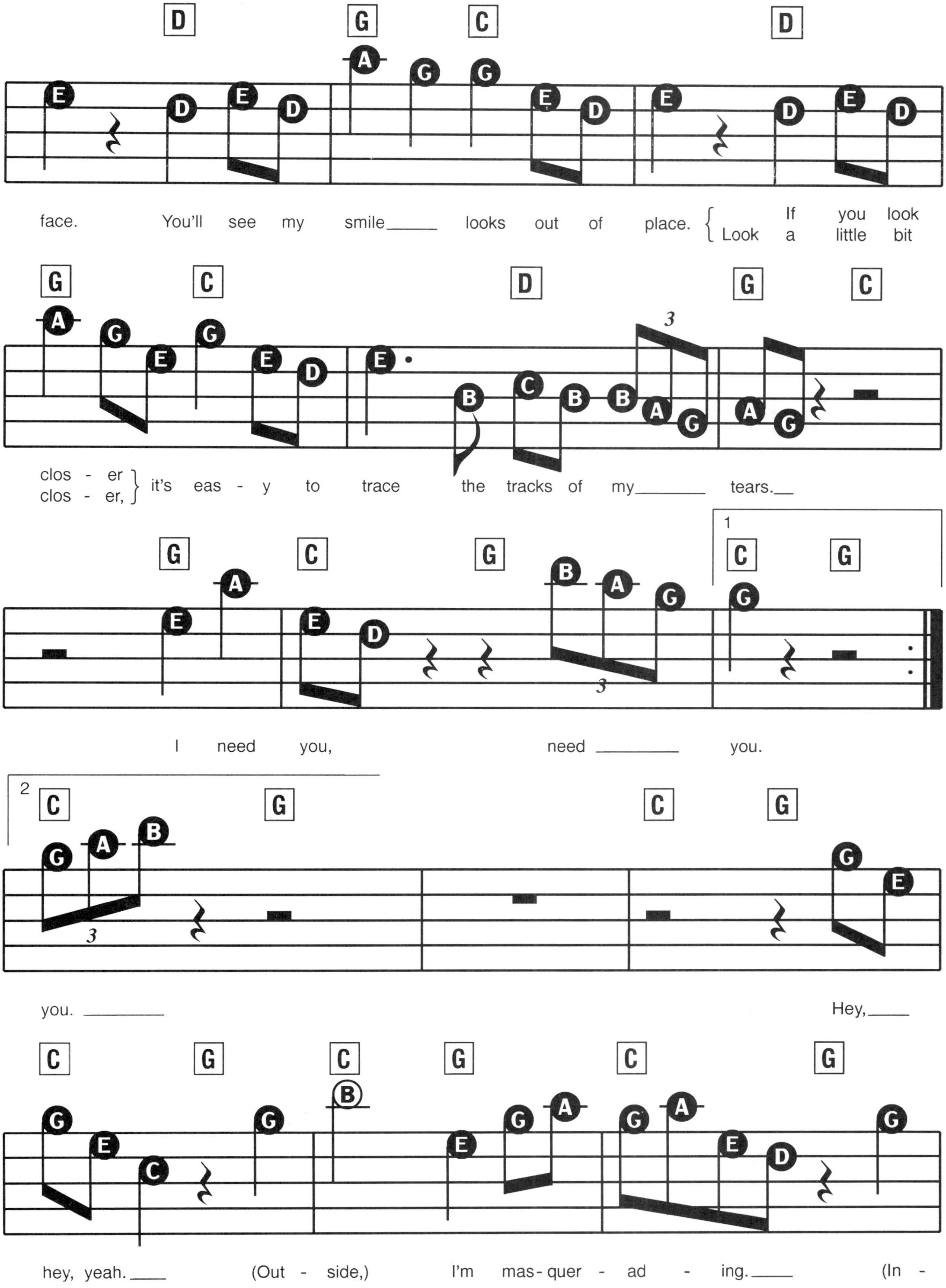
D G C D
face. You'll see my smile___ looks out of place. { If you look / Look a little bit
G C D G C
clos - er / clos - er, } it's eas - y to trace the tracks of my___ tears.__
G C G
1
C G
I need you, need ___ you.
2
C G C G
you. ___ Hey,___
C G C G C G
hey, yeah.___ (Out - side,) I'm mas-quer - ad - ing.___ (In -

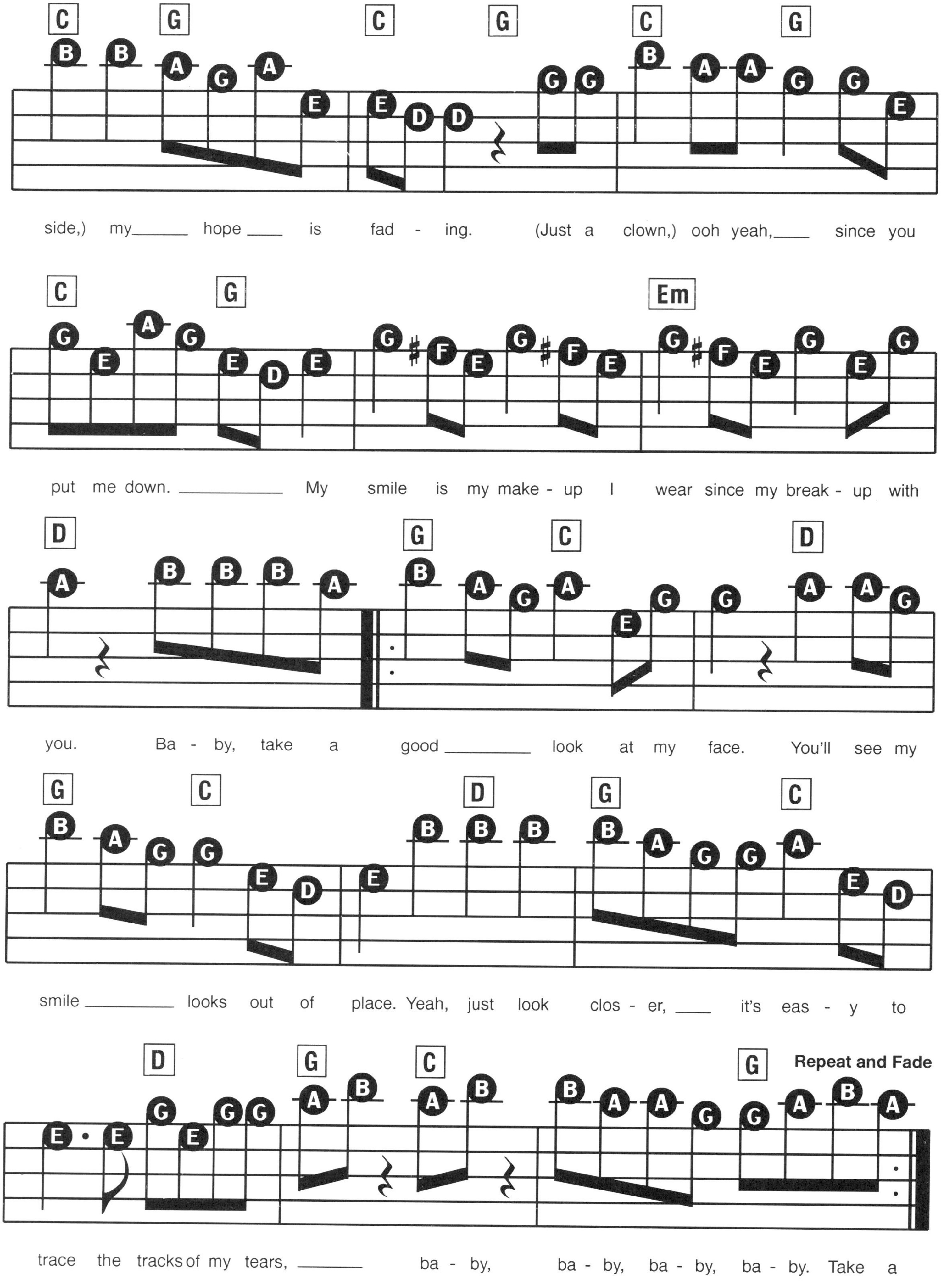
C G C G C G
side,) my hope is fad - ing. (Just a clown,) ooh yeah, since you
C G Em
put me down. My smile is my make - up I wear since my break - up with
D G C D
you. Ba - by, take a good look at my face. You'll see my
G C D G C
smile looks out of place. Yeah, just look clos - er, it's eas - y to
D G C G
Repeat and Fade
trace the tracks of my tears, ba - by, ba - by, ba - by, ba - by. Take a

You're All I Need to Get By

Registration 4
Rhythm: Pop

Words and Music by Nickolas Ashford
and Valerie Simpson

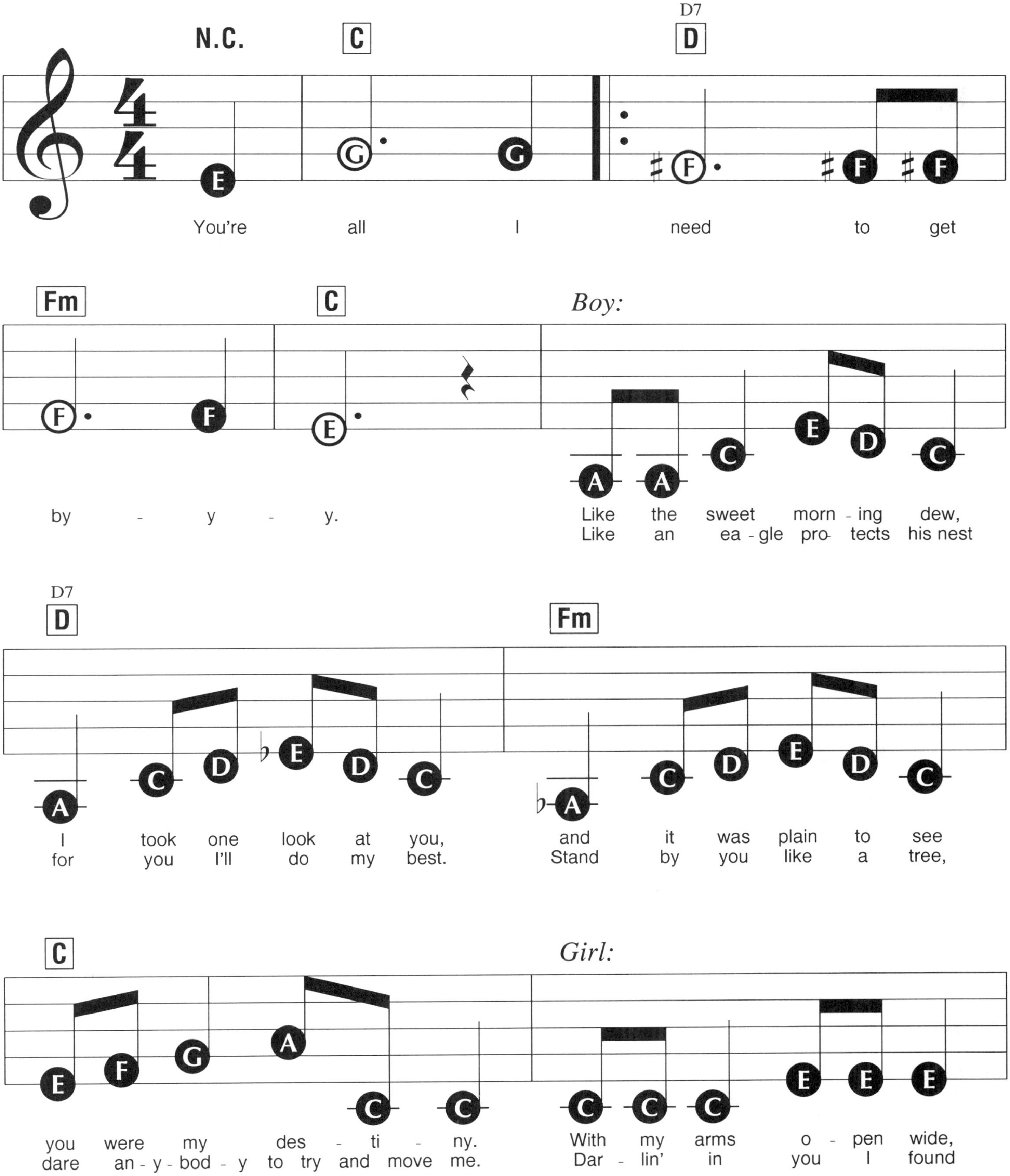

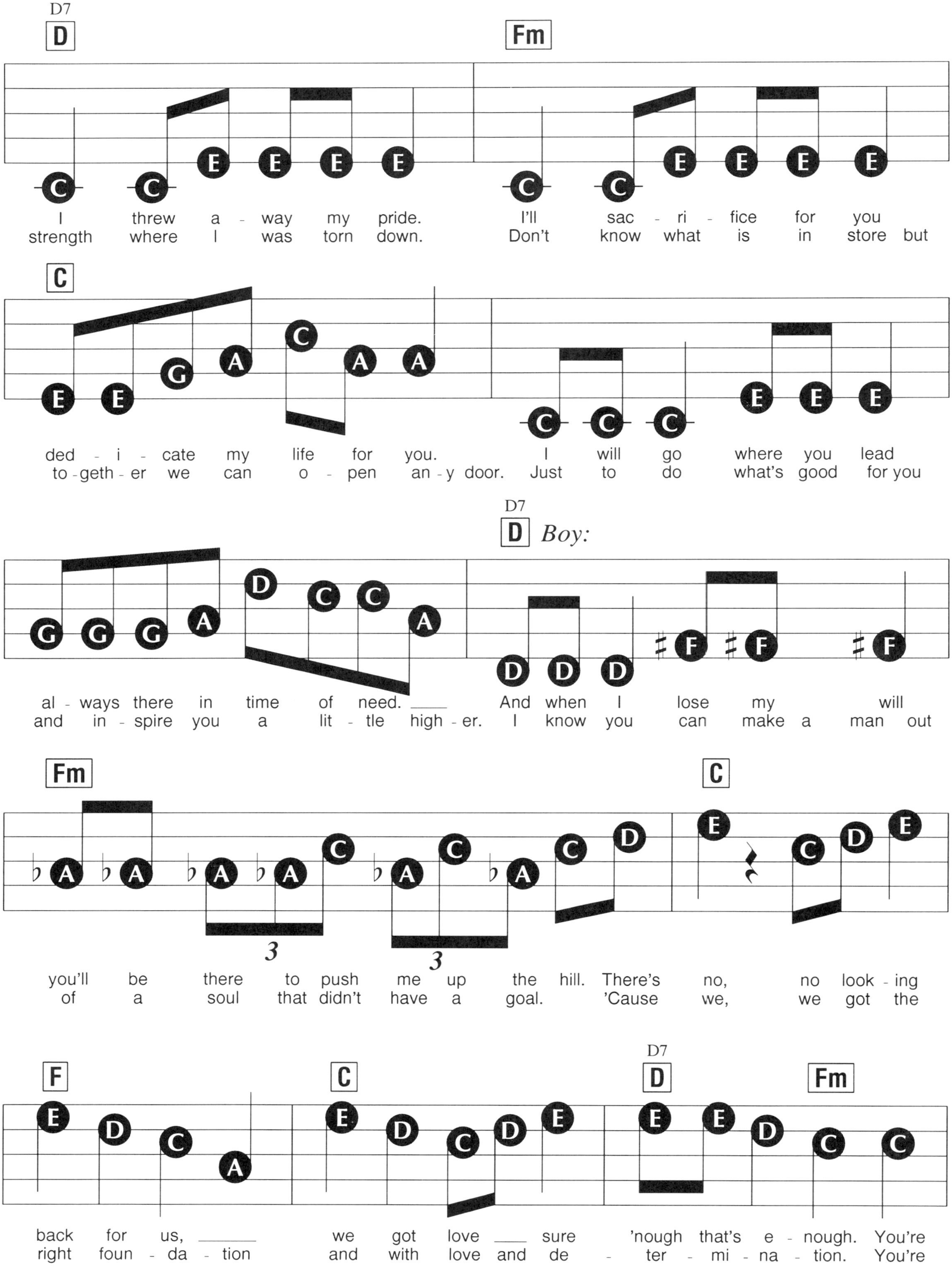
D7
D
Fm
C C E E E E
C C E E E E
I threw a - way my pride.
strength where I was torn down.
I'll sac - ri - fice for you
Don't know what is in store but
C
E E G A C A A
C C C E E E
ded - i - cate my life for you.
to - geth - er we can o - pen an - y door.
I will go where you lead
Just to do what's good for you
D7
D Boy:
G G G A D C C A
D D D F F F
al - ways there in time of need.
and in - spire you a lit - tle high - er.
And when I lose my will
I know you can make a man out
Fm
C
A A A A C A C A C D
E C D E
3
3
you'll be there to push me up the hill.
of a soul that didn't have a goal.
There's no, no look - ing
'Cause we, we got the
F
C
D7
D
Fm
E D C A
E D C D E
E E D C C
back for us,
right foun - da - tion
we got love sure
and with love and de - ter - mi - na - tion.
'nough that's e - nough. You're
You're

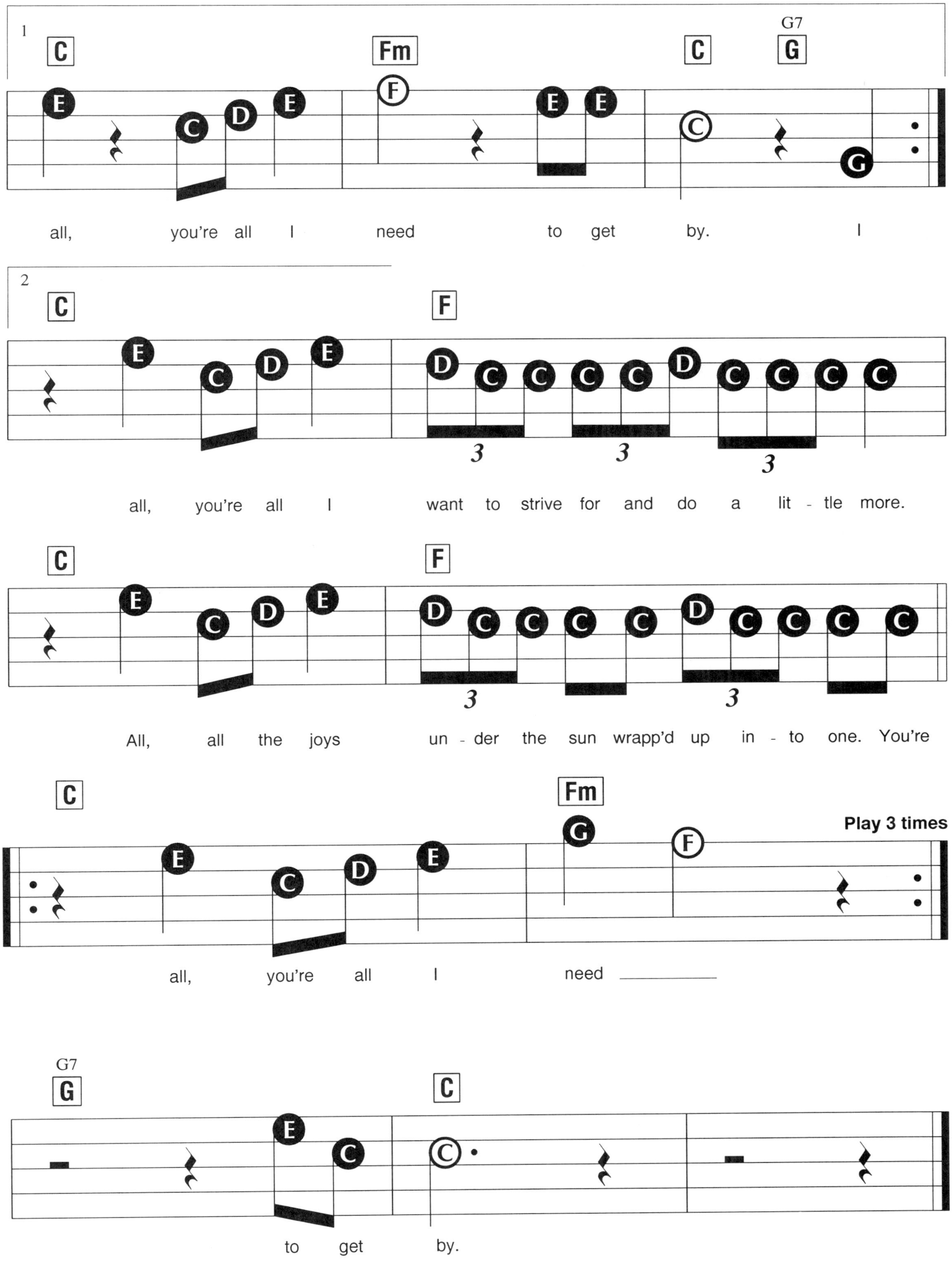
1
C Fm C G7 G
all, you're all I need to get by. I
2
C F
all, you're all I want to strive for and do a lit - tle more.
C F
All, all the joys un - der the sun wrapp'd up in - to one. You're
C Fm
Play 3 times
all, you're all I need
G7 G C
to get by.

What's Going On

Registration 7
Rhythm: Rock or 16 - Beat

Words and Music by Marvin Gaye,
Al Cleveland and Renaldo Benson

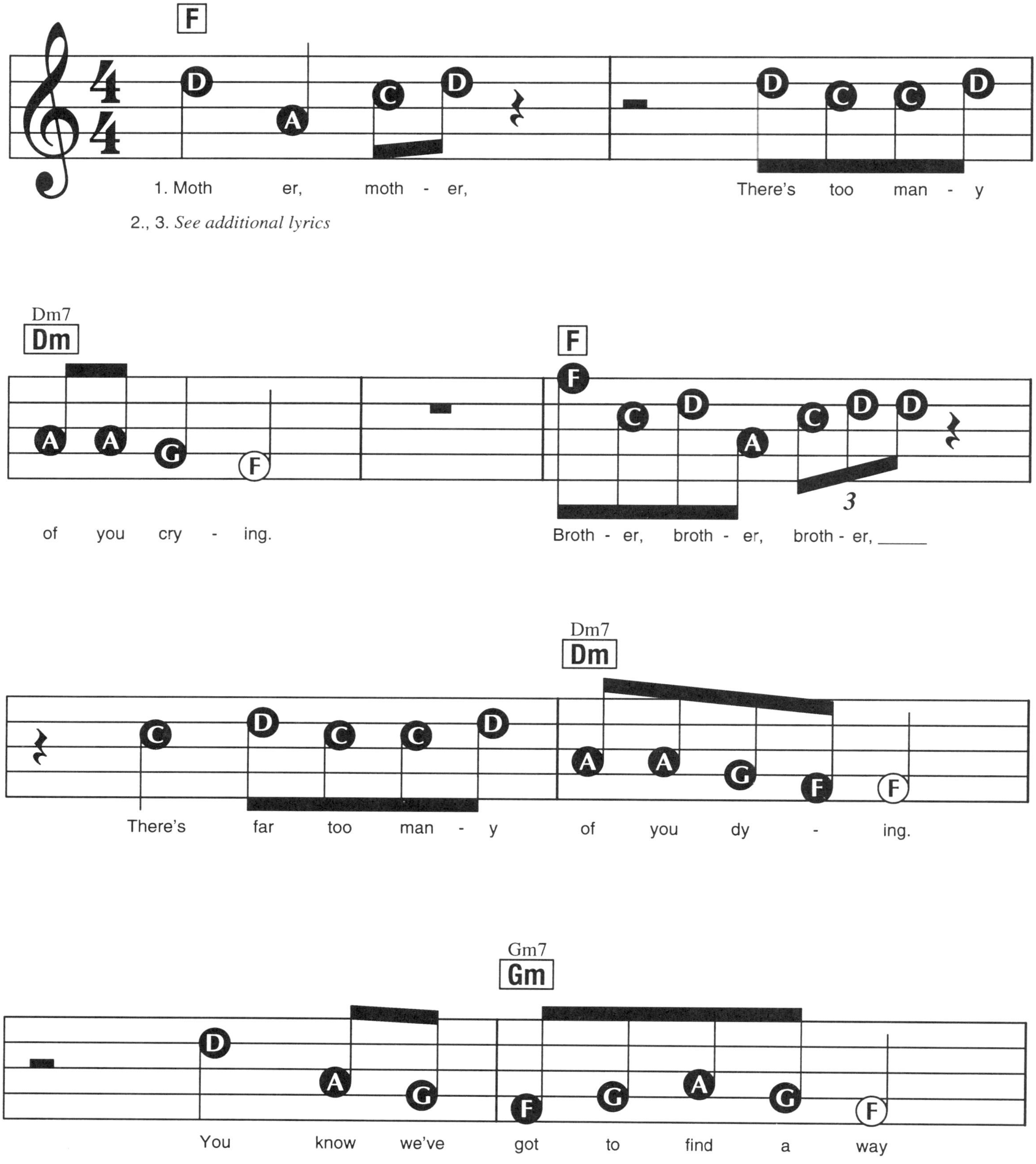

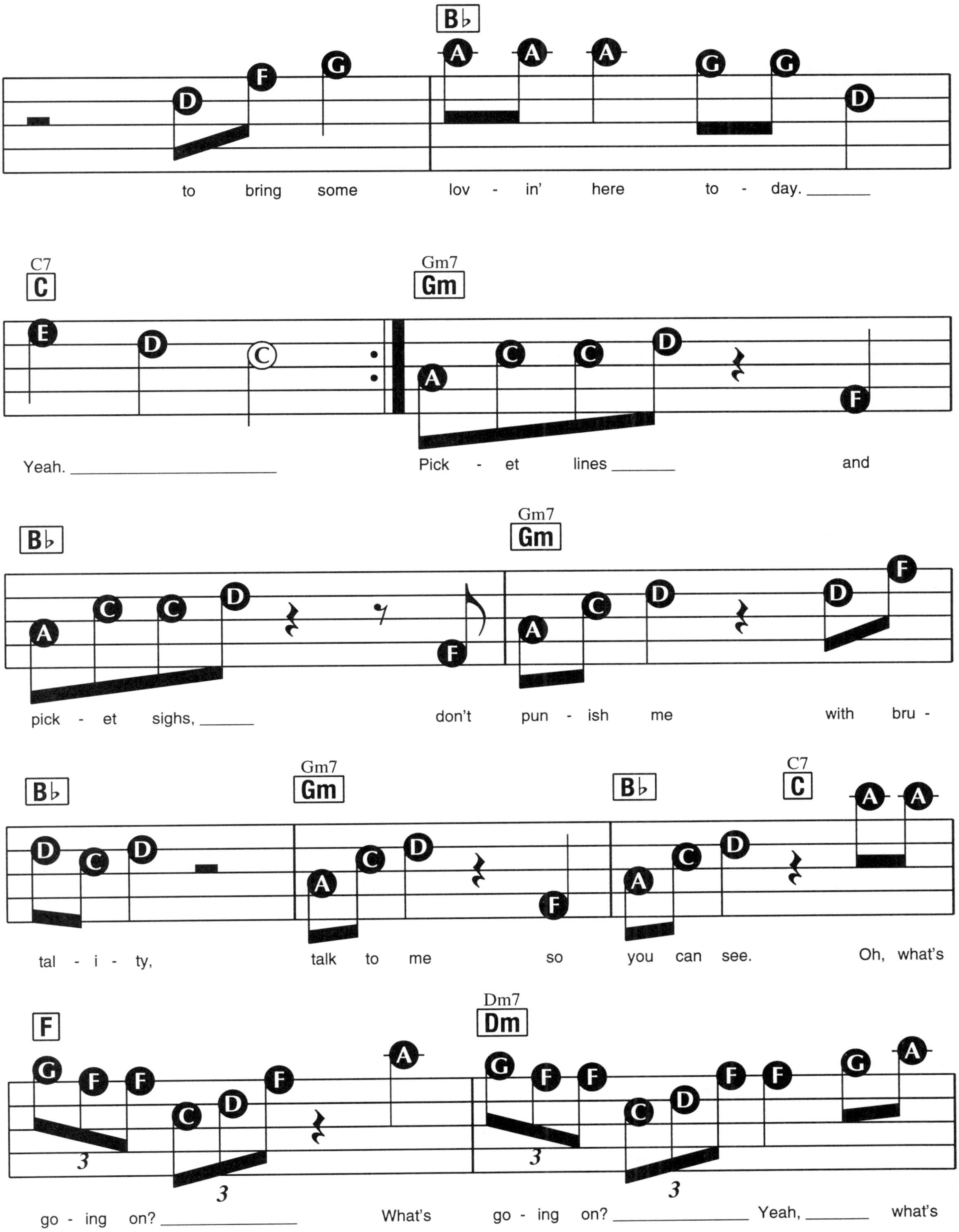
B♭
to bring some lov - in' here to - day.
C7 C
Gm7 Gm
Yeah.
Pick - et lines and
B♭
Gm7 Gm
pick - et sighs, don't pun - ish me with bru -
B♭
Gm7 Gm
B♭
C7 C
tal - i - ty, talk to me so you can see. Oh, what's
F
Dm7 Dm
go - ing on? What's go - ing on? Yeah, what's

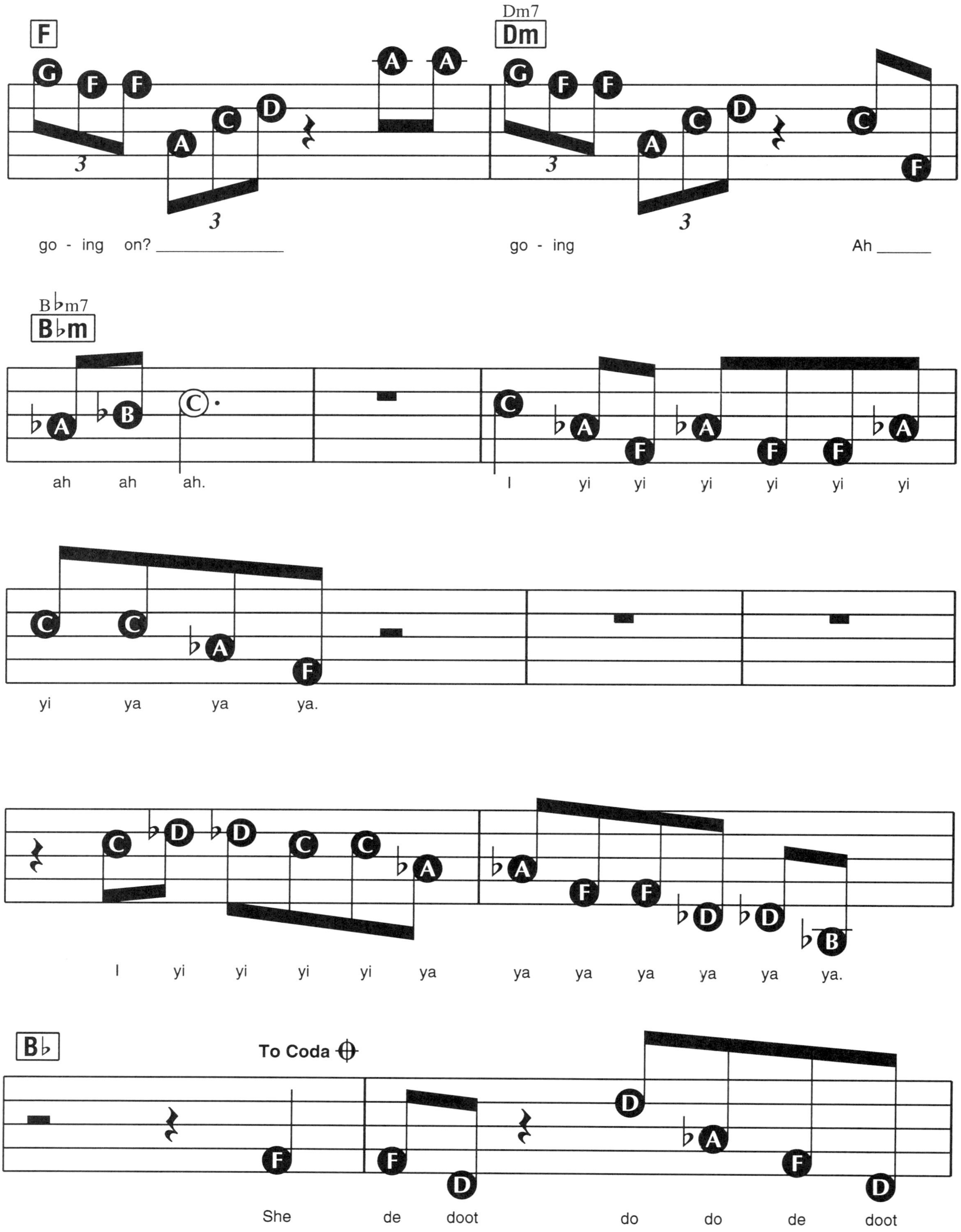
F
Dm7
Dm
go - ing on? ______________
go - ing
Ah ______
B♭m7
B♭m
ah ah ah.
I yi yi yi yi yi yi
yi ya ya ya.
I yi yi yi yi ya
ya ya ya ya ya ya.
B♭
To Coda
She
de doot
do do de doot

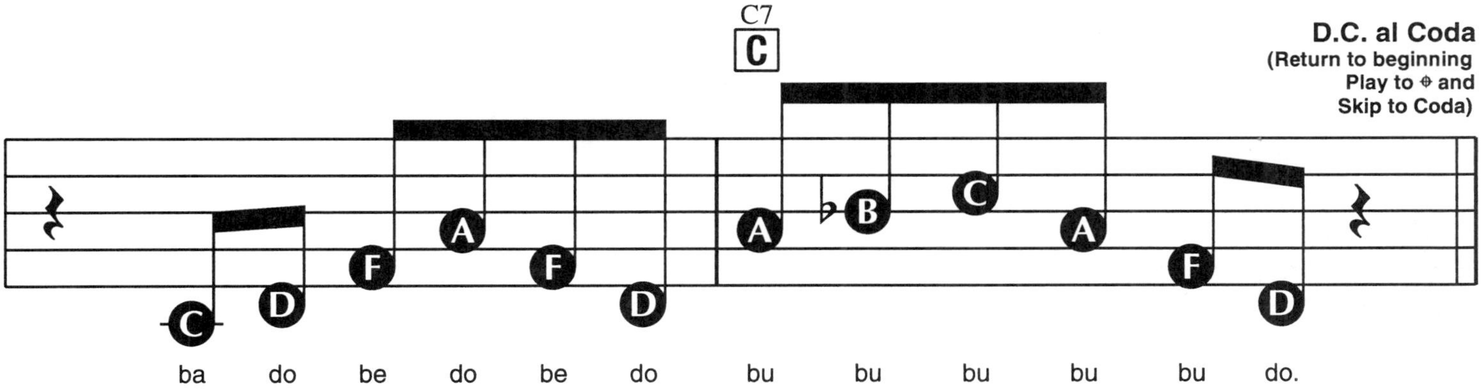

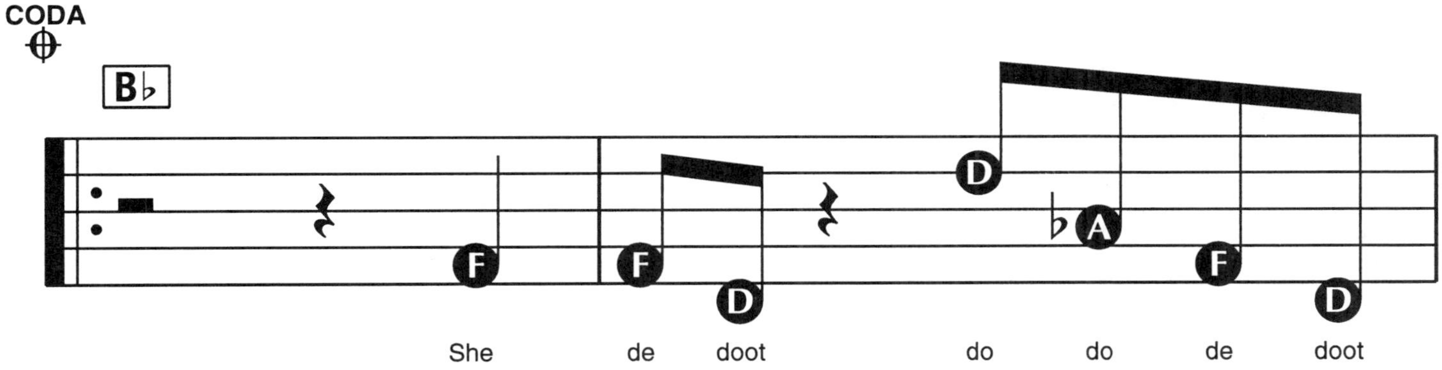

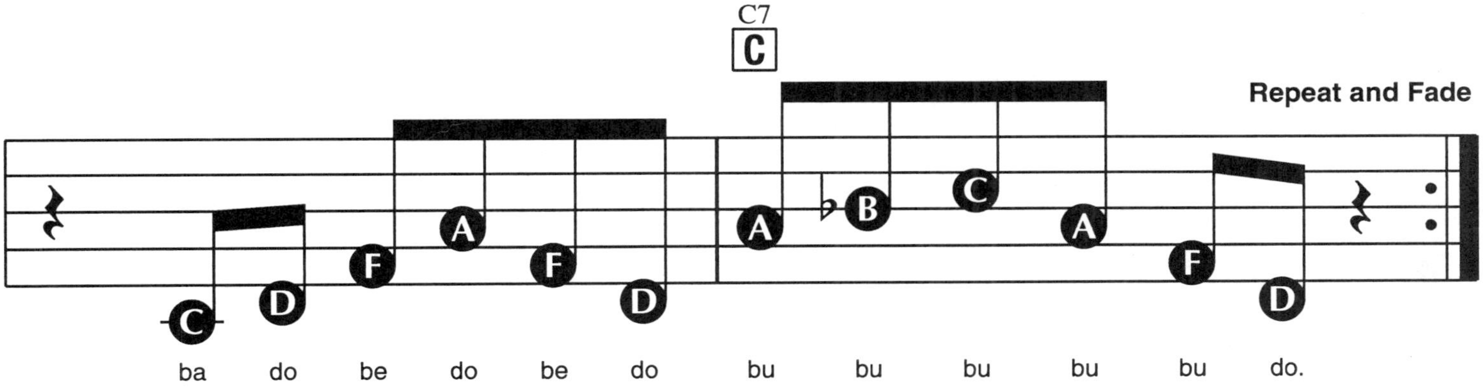

Additional Lyrics

2. Father, father, we don't need to escalate,
You see, war is not the answer, for only love can conquer hate.
You know we've got to find a way to bring some lovin' here today. *(Chorus)*

3. Father, father, everybody thinks we're wrong.
Oh but, who are they to judge us simply because our hair is long?
Oh, you know we've got to find a way bring some understanding here today. *(Chorus)*

Where Did Our Love Go

Registration 2
Rhythm: Swing or Shuffle

Words and Music by Brian Holland,
Lamont Dozier and Edward Holland

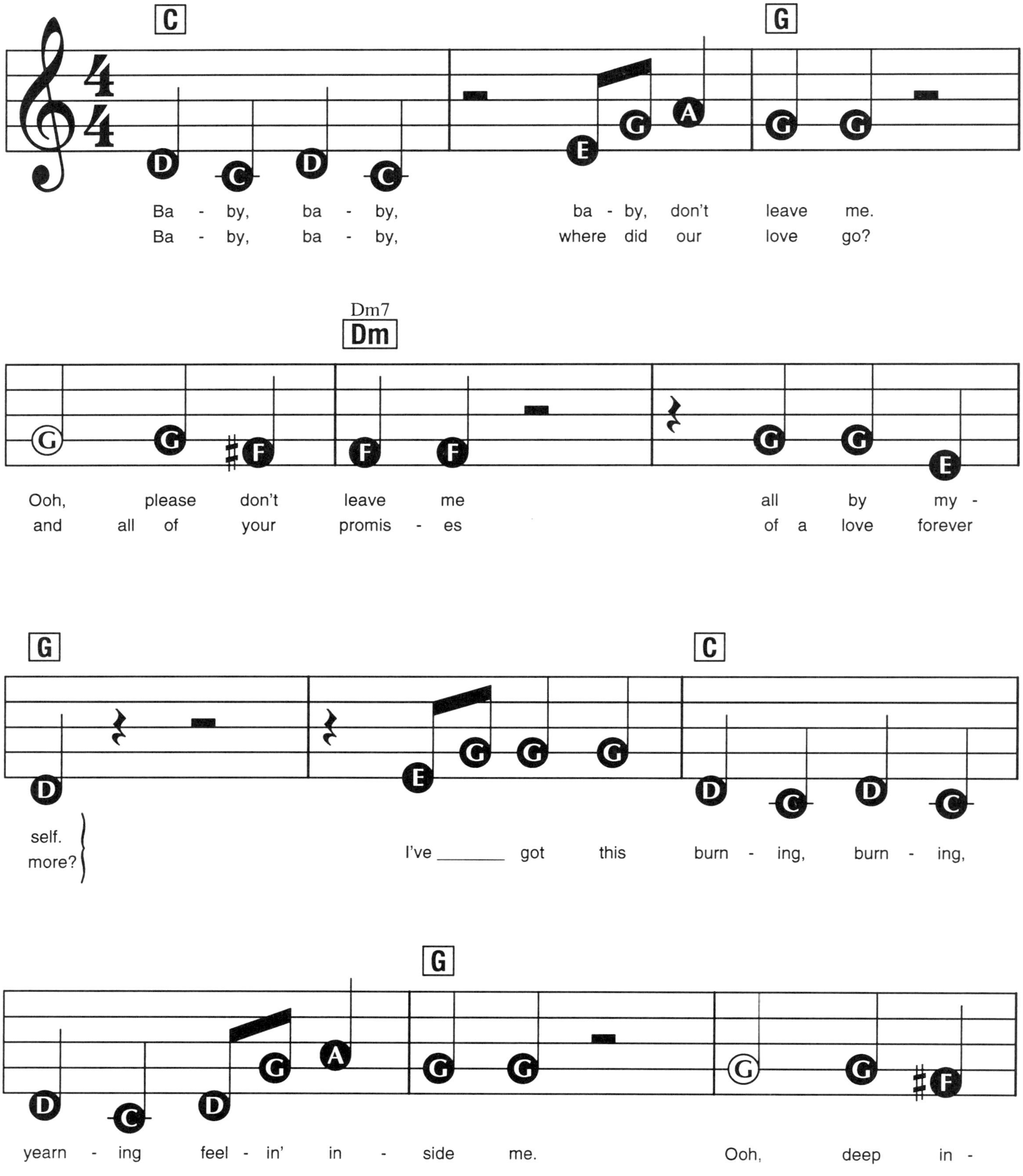

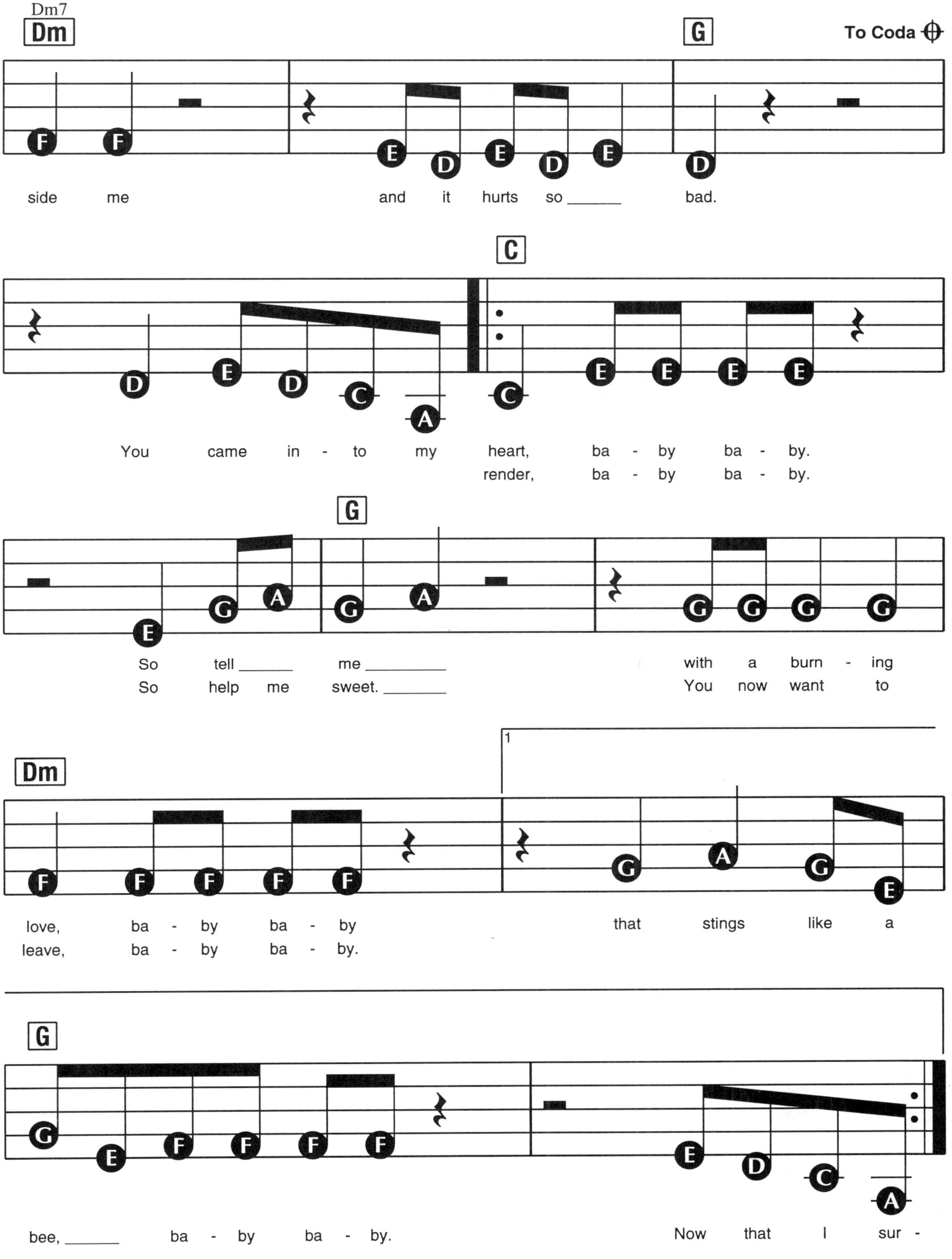

Dm7
Dm
G
To Coda
side me and it hurts so bad.
C
You came in - to my heart, ba - by ba - by.
render, ba - by ba - by.
G
So tell me with a burn - ing
So help me sweet. You now want to
Dm
1
love, ba - by ba - by that stings like a
leave, ba - by ba - by.
G
bee, ba - by ba - by. Now that I sur -

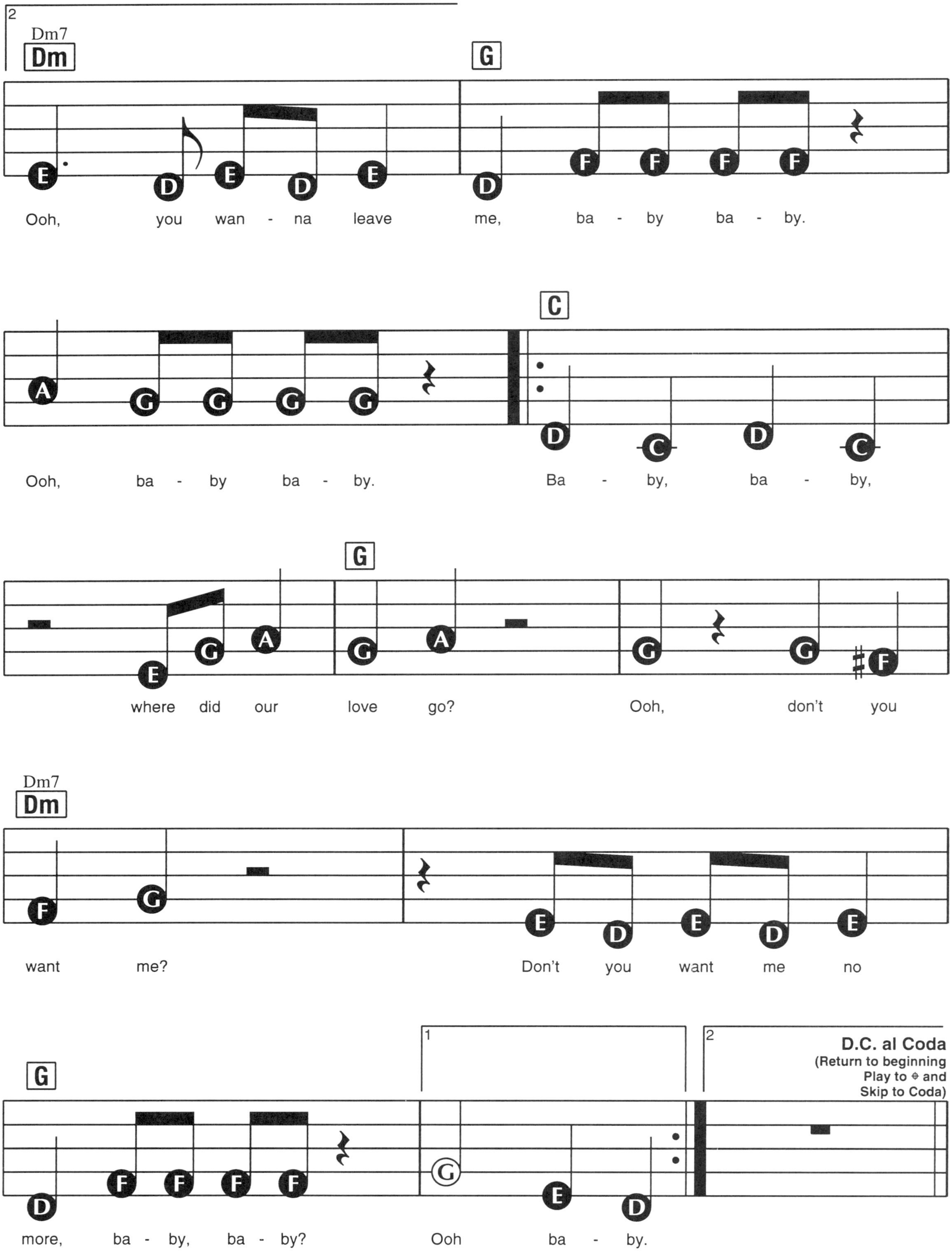
2
Dm7
Dm
E D E D E
Ooh, you wan - na leave
G
D F F F F
me, ba - by ba - by.
A G G G G
Ooh, ba - by ba - by.
C
D C D C
Ba - by, ba - by,
E G A
where did our
G
G A
love go?
G G F
Ooh, don't you
Dm7
Dm
F G
want me?
E D E D E
Don't you want me no
G
D F F F F
more, ba - by, ba - by?
1
G E D
Ooh ba - by.
2
D.C. al Coda
(Return to beginning
Play to ⊕ and
Skip to Coda)

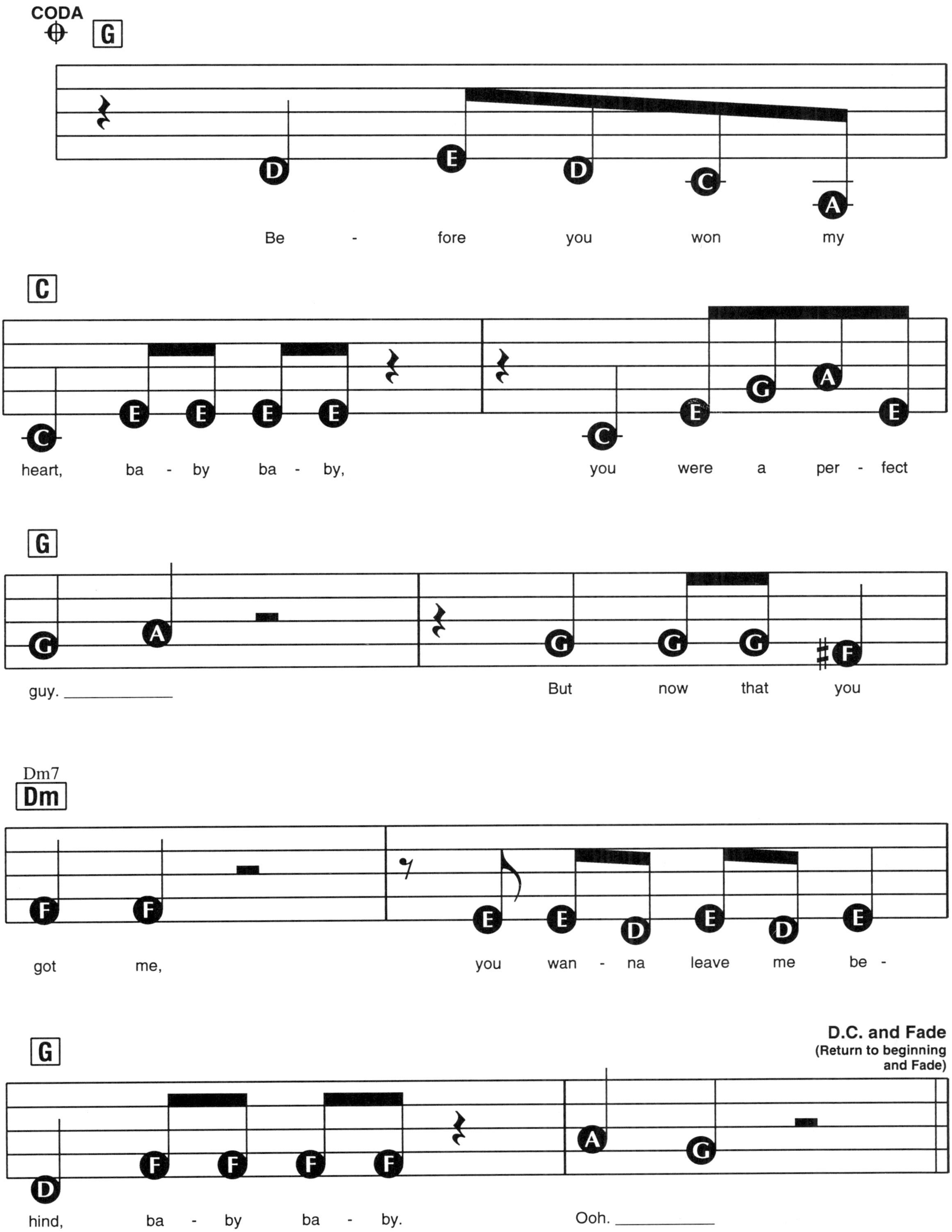
CODA
G
Be - fore you won my
C
heart, ba - by ba - by, you were a per - fect
G
guy. But now that you
Dm7
Dm
got me, you wan - na leave me be -
G
hind, ba - by ba - by. Ooh.
D.C. and Fade
(Return to beginning and Fade)

You've Really Got a Hold on Me

Registration 8
Rhythm: Slow Rock

Words and Music by
William "Smokey" Robinson

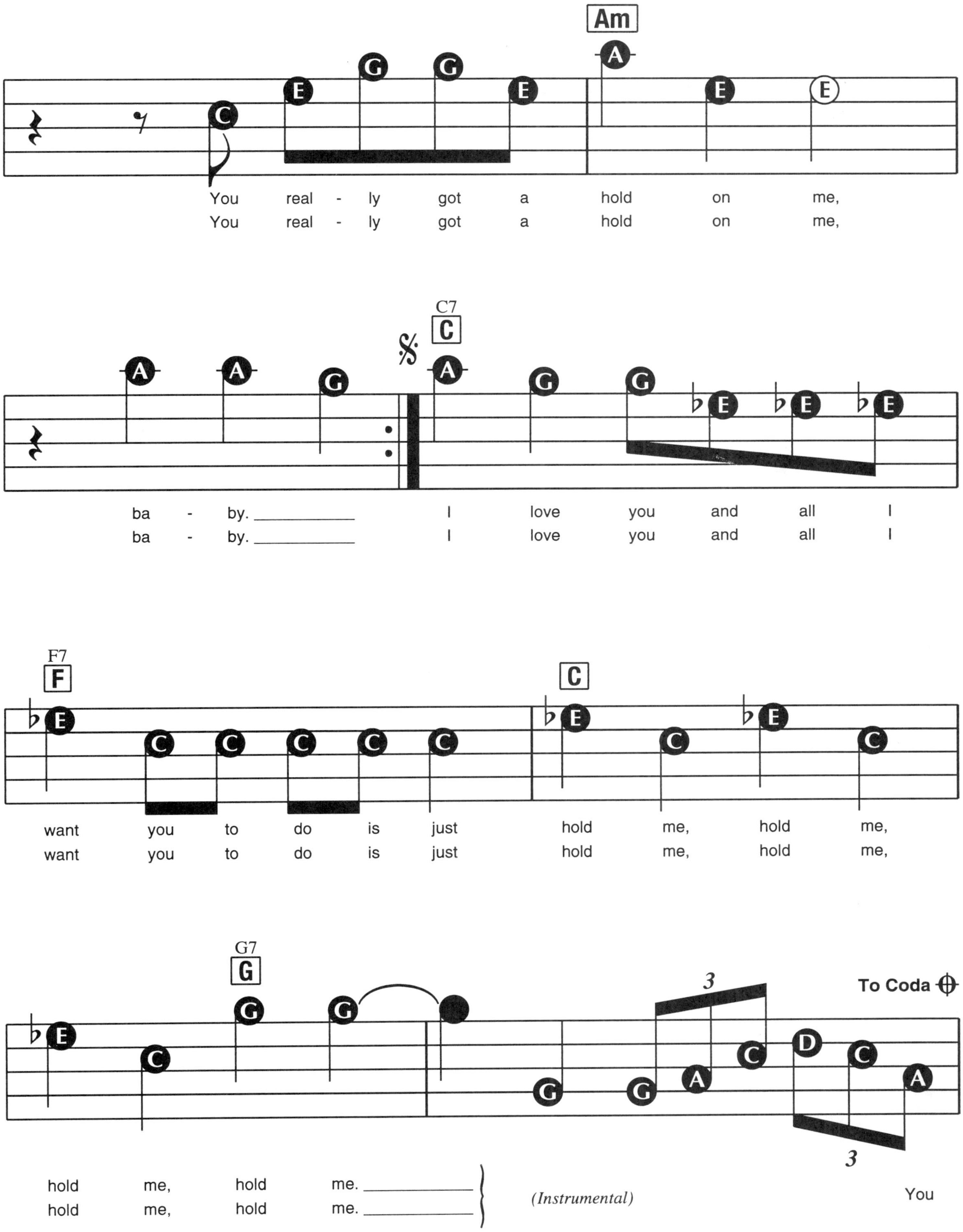
Am
C E G G E A E E
You real - ly got a hold on me,
You real - ly got a hold on me,
C7
C
A A G A G G E E E
ba - by. I love you and all I
ba - by. I love you and all I
F7
F
C
E C C C C C E C E C
want you to do is just hold me, hold me,
want you to do is just hold me, hold me,
G7
G
E C G G G G A C D C A
3
3
To Coda
hold me, hold me.
hold me, hold me.
(Instrumental)
You

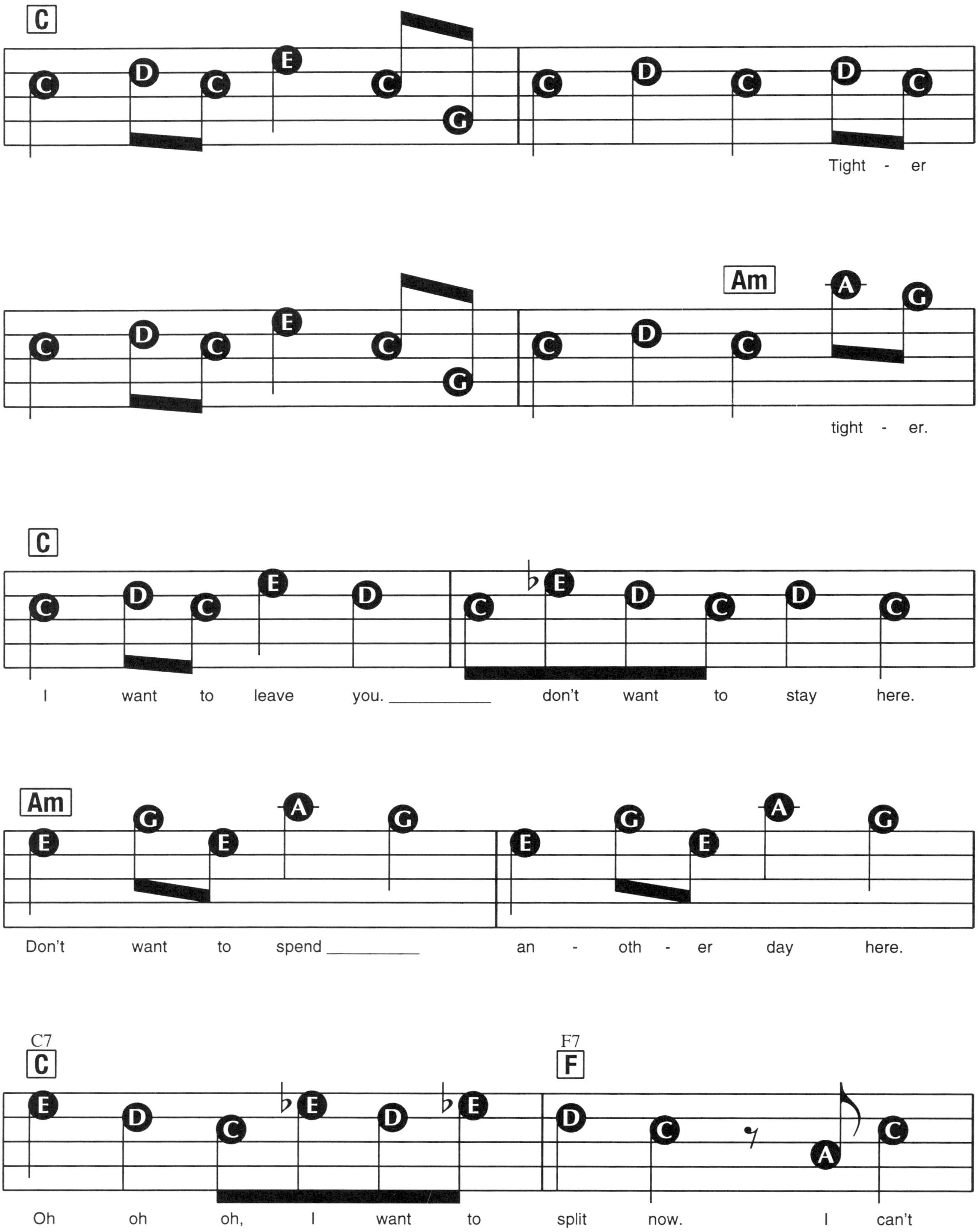
C
Tight - er
Am
tight - er.
C
I want to leave you. ___ don't want to stay here.
Am
Don't want to spend ___ an - oth - er day here.
C7
C
F7
F
Oh oh oh, I want to split now. I can't

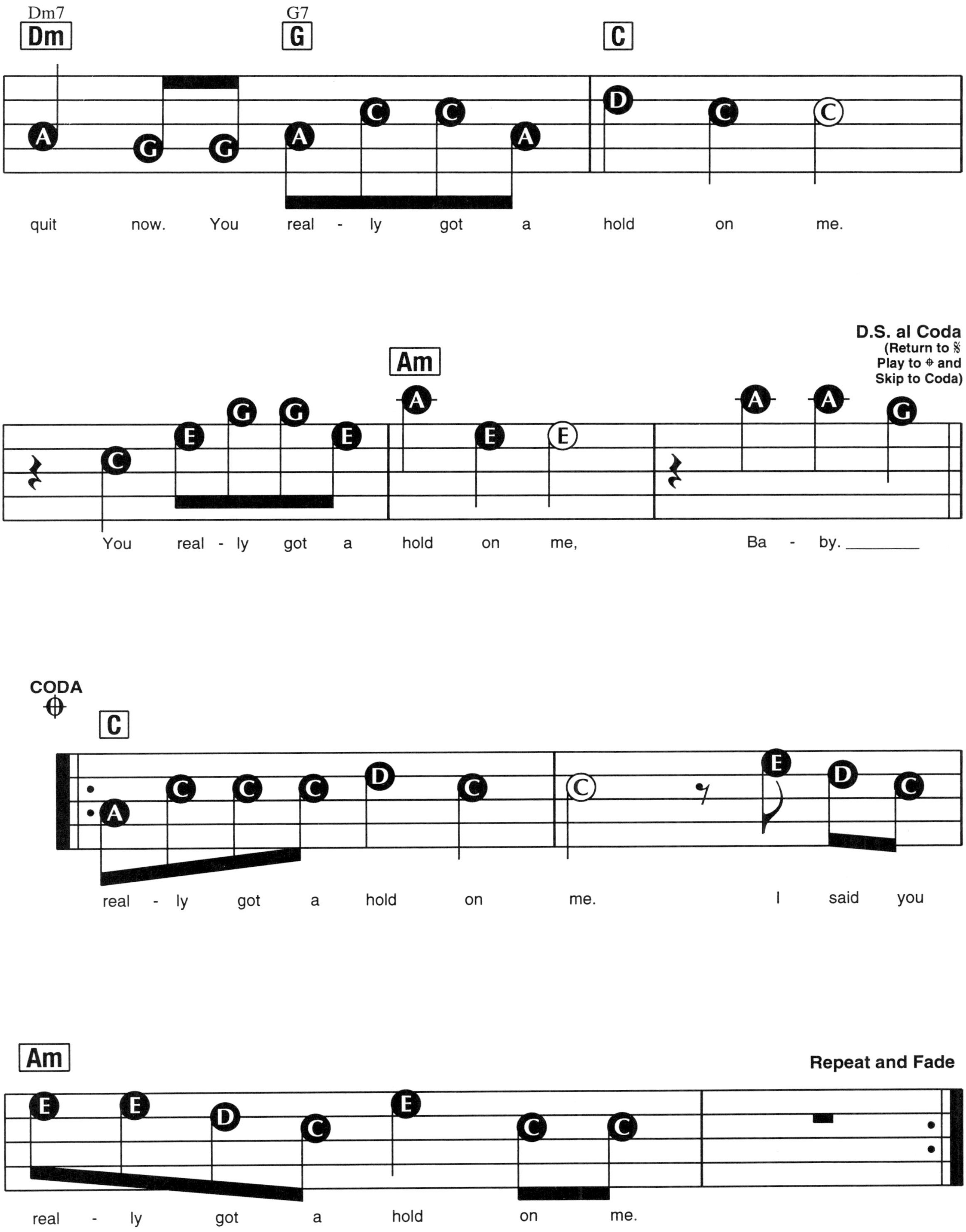
Dm7
Dm
G7
G
C
quit now. You real - ly got a hold on me.
Am
D.S. al Coda
(Return to 𝄋
Play to ⊕ and
Skip to Coda)
You real - ly got a hold on me, Ba - by.
CODA
C
real - ly got a hold on me. I said you
Am
Repeat and Fade
real - ly got a hold on me.

You've Made Me So Very Happy

Registration 1
Rhythm: Rock or 8 Beat

Words and Music by Berry Gordy, Frank Wilson,
Brenda Holloway and Patrice Holloway

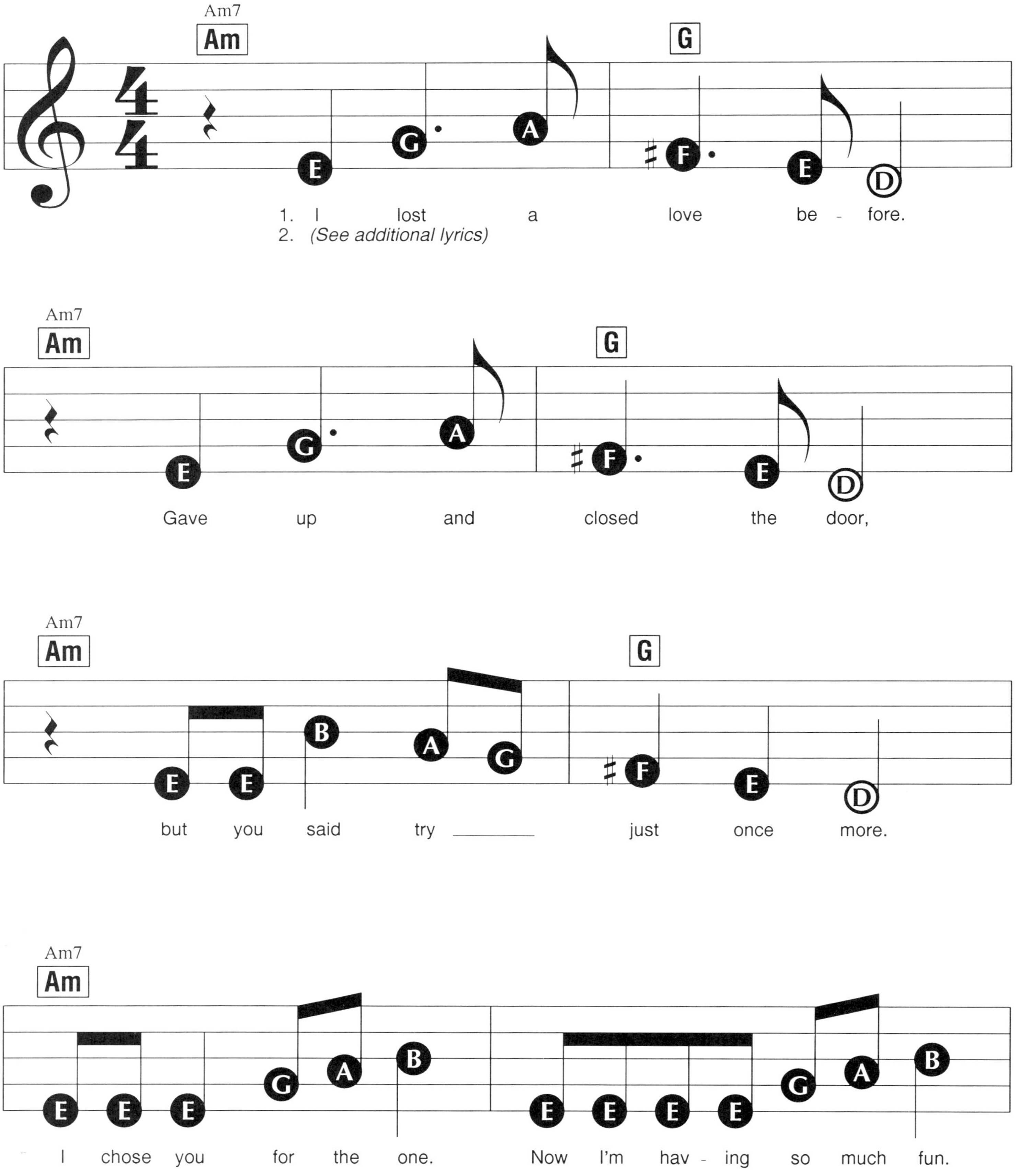

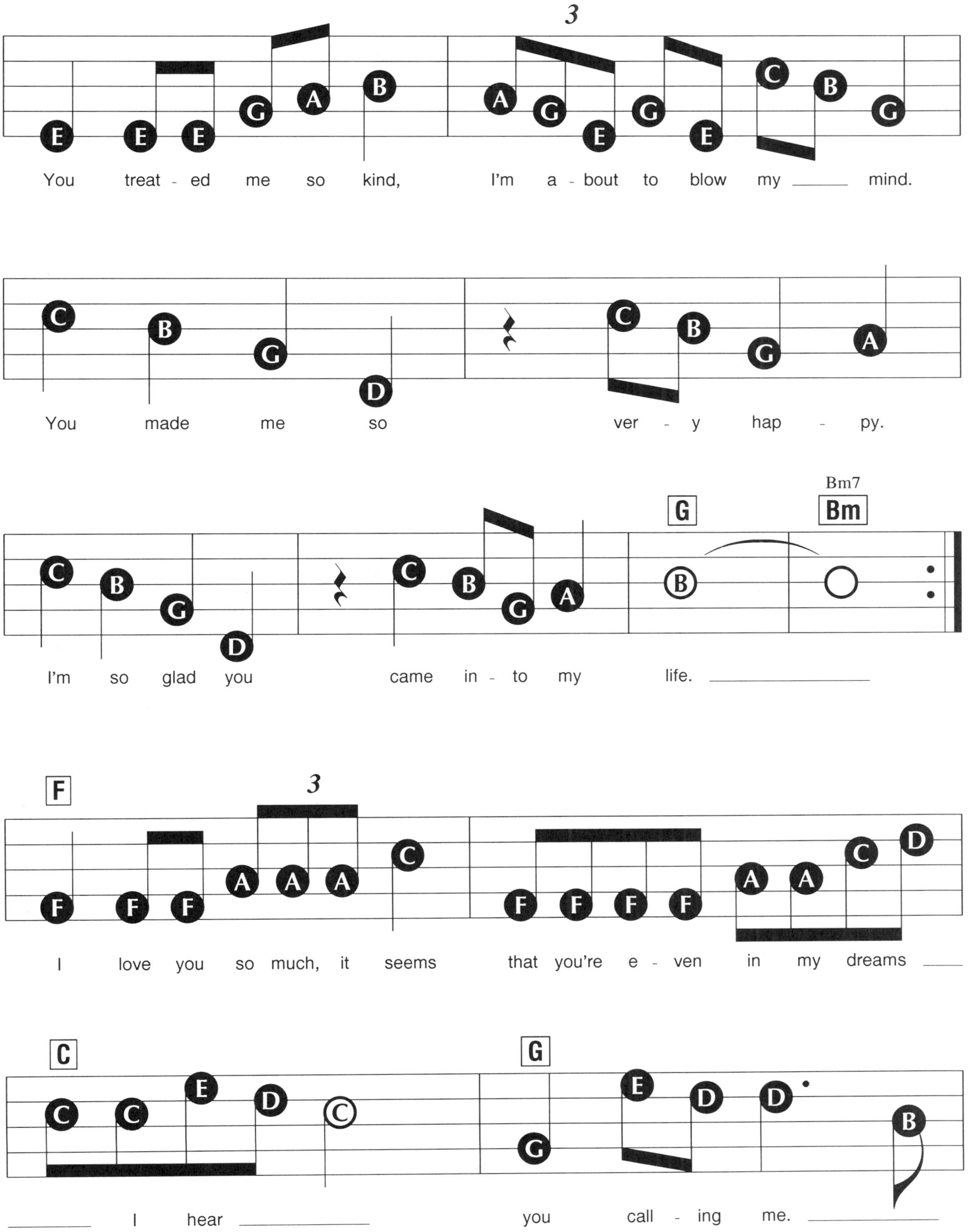
You treat - ed me so kind, I'm a - bout to blow my mind.
You made me so ver - y hap - py.
G
Bm7
Bm
I'm so glad you came in - to my life.
F
I love you so much, it seems that you're e - ven in my dreams
C
G
I hear you call - ing me.

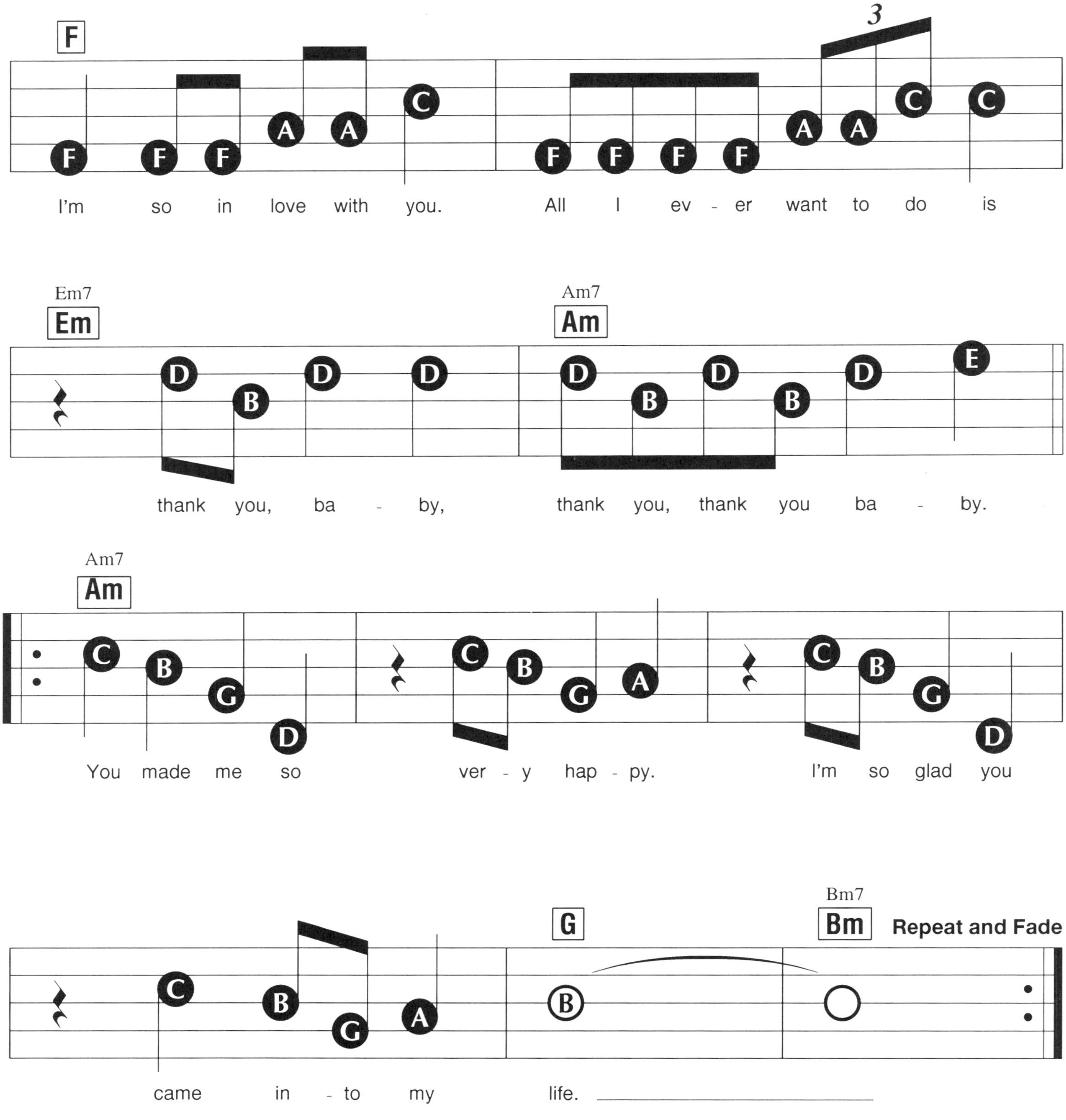

Additional Lyrics

2. The others were untrue, but when it came to you,
   I'd spend my whole life with you.
   'Cause you came and took control,
   You touched my very soul.
   You always showed me that loving you was where it's at.